CW01466469

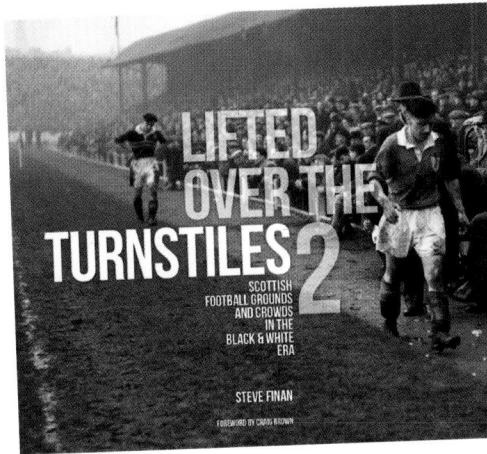

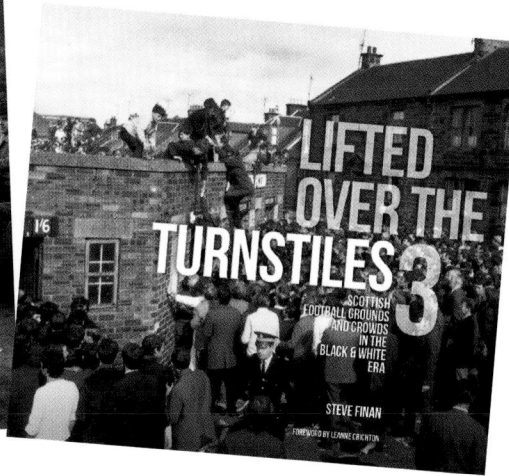

BY STEVE FINAN

There are two linked volumes of these latest Lifted Over The Turnstiles books, with Scotland's teams spread equally over them. To purchase the other volume go to: www.dcthomsonshop.co.uk

Volume 2: ISBN 978-1-84535-889-1

First published in Great Britain in 2021 by DC Thomson & Co., Ltd., Meadowside, Dundee, DD1 9QJ.

Copyright © DC Thomson & Co., Limited.

All rights reserved. No part of this publication may be reproduced, stored in a retrieval system, or transmitted by any means, without the prior permission in writing of the copyright holder, nor be otherwise circulated in any form of binding or cover other than that in which it is published. This book is sold on the condition that it — and especially the photos within it — will not, by way of trade or otherwise, be posted online, resold, hired out, lent or otherwise distributed, or circulated in any form or style.

Main text Copyright © 2021 DC Thomson & Co., Ltd.

Compiling these books has been the most enjoyable and rewarding task of my working life.
I am immensely proud of them. I therefore dedicate both books to the most important people
in my life, my wife, daughter and son – Carole, Rebecca and Lewis Finan.

COVER/BACK COVER DESIGN | LEON STRACHAN

Typeset, internal design and composition by Steve Finan (proudly a hot metal compositor 1979-83).

This book is set in Times New Roman regular/bold/italic 13 point on 15.6 point leading.

The photos in this book are available to buy from
www.photoshopscotland.co.uk

Introduction

THE success of the first *Lifted Over The Turnstiles* volume was a pleasant surprise.

Perhaps it shouldn't have been, because everyone knows that the affection football fans have for their grounds is immense.

However, my pleasure at the reception given to the book was tempered by a smidgeon of guilt. I knew I could do better.

The first volume of Turnstiles was full of interesting photos and I was very proud of it. But at the same time I knew that in the DC Thomson archive there was much more to find.

For the first book I'd mainly looked at the store of developed-from-negatives photos. But there were thousands, tens of thousands, of photos that had never been developed. Some were 35mm film, many others were glass plate negatives.

It has taken a while, indeed nearly four years, to sift through them.

And I was right. There were real gems. So many that it wasn't easy to choose. For some of the games there were 70 or 80 photos taken. Deciding which to show – this great shot with the stand in the background, or this with one of the most famous names in the club's history in the foreground – was very difficult.

That in-depth strength of material is why there are two books, the grounds are split over Volumes 2 and 3. The original plan was for just one book, but that wouldn't have been nearly enough. There followed some frankly unfeasible discussions about putting out a 700-page book. But the solution was to put out two books, each of 360 pages.

Almost every Scottish ground is featured.

Working with negatives, though, throws up a repeated problem. When I did find a good photo, too often it would have very little information stored with it. That's when the success of Turnstiles 1 paid off.

Since doing that book I have been getting out to speak to Football Memories groups all over Scotland. And I must pay tribute to the people who run these events, they are highly enjoyable.

But I'd thought that these visits were something I could do to help others – my own (long dead) father would have enjoyed participating in these groups when he first began to suffer memory problems.

It turned out to be the other way around. I wasn't helping them, they were helping me.

I'd show a slide of an old stadium, which would start a discussion. Experiences, facts, and reminiscences would tumble out. The Memories Groups' collective gimlet eye would point out things in the photos I had barely noticed, or not realised the significance of.

It soon transpired that I wasn't telling stories or handing out information – they were. The greatest store of football information that exists in this country isn't in books, archives or libraries, it is held in the memories of those who were there, those who stood on the terraces and sat in the grandstands.

I freely admit, indeed I celebrate the fact, that I have cultivated this knowledge. I have developed friendships among the older supporters of clubs all around the country who I can send a photo to, and who come back to me with fantastic, insightful, amazing information.

I regard these men as heroes. I stand in awe of their knowledge. I am humbled by how much they know and embarrassed by how little I know.

This became the best, the most enjoyable, project I've ever undertaken. I kept finding amazing photos, and had great fun discussing and unravelling what I was looking at with my widely-dispersed teams of experts.

In this Volume 2, I was mesmerised by the Hampden photo on pages 120-121. I sat gazing at it for a full hour, remembering where I'd stood for the big games. The Tannadice pavilion (p258), Dens under lights (274), and the wide vista of Central Park (318) also gripped me.

My favourite, though, is the wide panorama of Brockville on pages 154-155. Brockville is gone, it is now a supermarket. A new photo of the old place is a genuine piece of Scottish history unearthed.

I have spent more time and given more space to grounds that have disappeared. Brockville, Shawfield, Cathkin Park and Boghead in this book; Annfield, Muirton, Broomfield and Love Street in Volume 3. These places are the scenes of youth for older supporters, and almost mythical lands to younger fans. I am proud to have added to the canon of photos

Similarly, for stadiums that do still exist, I have concentrated on parts of them that have disappeared.

Many of the photos have play going on in the foreground, with views of the stands and terraces behind. I very much like this as it shows the football ground fulfilling its purpose. A good shot of a terrace, with a hero of the club in front, became the holy grail. Those are the photos I have sought out with most vigour, and which I came to value most.

Lastly, you fill find as you go through the book that I refer often to the work of the great stadium designer Archibald Leitch (1865-1939). Better writers than me have outlined the career of this Glasgow-born genius and his legacy on British football. I have sought merely to show off his work in Scotland.

Steve Finan 2021

Foreword, by Craig Brown

VERY sadly it has taken a worldwide pandemic to make many of us appreciate what crowds do for football. For more than a year the game at the top level had to be played with no spectators permitted.

Although the medical advice had to be respected and adhered to, there is absolutely no doubt that it was far from the same matchday experience having to watch games on television. The absence of spectators made everyone appreciate crowds at football matches.

In this superb publication, Steve's unrivalled collection of photos of the traditional grounds of the 1950s, 60s and 70s, fully or even partially attended, bring back poignant memories for me.

I had the good fortune to play for three teams in that era, manage three teams slightly later and, significantly, work with the National Team for 15 years where the majority of home matches were located at Hampden.

Indeed we even had a 52,000 crowd there for a youth match, the FIFA World Cup Final, Scotland v Saudi Arabia, following a semi-final victory against Portugal at Tynecastle with 27,000 inside – and a further couple of thousand locked out.

Like Steve, I have a fascination for football grounds beginning with the quaint charm of Douglas Park, the home of Hamilton Academical FC, or "The Accies" as they were affectionately called.

I was a ball boy there in the 1950s when Jackie Cox was manager. A new ball was required for the start of every game so, before the time of sponsorship, the manager's instruction was to get it quickly to Bobby Shearer who booted it over the main stand, necessitating a used replacement. I, or one of my pals, was positioned to recover what became the "new" ball for the next home match. The sooner Bobby got it over the stand to me the more of the game I saw!

Across the Clyde, was another of my favourite stadiums, that of Motherwell FC. I remember when I was assistant manager there in the mid-1970s and the late, great Jock Stein brought his Celtic team, Kenny Dalglish et al, for a Scottish Cup match which, incidentally, the home side won! There was a love/hate relationship with Mr Stein and the 'Well groundsman, Andy Russell, and when he asked Andy the condition of the playing surface, the reply from the venerable groundsman was, "Guid enough for what's goin' on to it!" Not the kind of response to endear himself to Celtic's greatest ever manager.

Most of my experiences at games have been as player or manager and I have to admit that I much prefer the grounds like Celtic Park, Easter Road, Fir Park, Fountain of Youth Stadium, Global Energy Stadium, Hampden, Ibrox, McDiarmid Park, or Tynecastle, where the teams enter and leave at the middle of the ground and there is no requirement to "walk the plank" from a corner to the technical area or dugout.

It's not comfortable to have to walk 50 yards or more when losing at half-time or after a defeat at Dens Park, East End Park, Pittodrie, Stark's Park, Tannadice or even the slightly shorter distance at Rugby Park. Nor was there much fun at the former ground of Clyde FC, Shawfield Stadium, where, for nine years, we had to walk across the dog track to get to the dressing room.

Whatever the configuration of the stadium there will be fans who like to have ready access to the players and respective managers.

Steve has brilliantly depicted the visuals of the venues but obviously not the auditory aspect.

As someone who loves the humour in the game I add a few instances of crowd involvement, some spontaneous and involuntary, some clearly rehearsed possibly on the supporters' bus driving to the match.

There's praise which is pleasant. There's abuse which is unpleasant. As a player at Falkirk FC's Brockville Stadium I was told, "Broon, you're rubbish. C'mon up here and watch yersel!"

At the same venue when, again, I was being told how hopeless I was and what a horrible game it was, I made the mistake of talking to the loudmouth by shouting, "You're the mug. You paid to get in!" Quick as a flash he buried me with the retort, "But you'll be ##### payin' next season!" I didn't know it at the time, but the guy was a prophet!

From the crowd there are compliments and there is criticism. That's expected. However, often there is humour. That's delightful.

During a game at Fir Park, Motherwell v Aberdeen, the visiting team captain, Willie Miller, who was disposed to offer unsolicited assistance to the match officials, received a severe injury which required a lengthy spell of treatment. A wag from the packed enclosure shouted, "Haw ref, Miller's injured. You're on your own now!"

You won't be alone looking at this marvellous collection of photographic treasures.

There's so much history embedded in the scenes. At Pittodrie, for example, the Beach End is where the first ever British knee-slide was performed by Joe Harper – initially by accident on the slippy surface.

The demand thereafter from the fans was such that this was his trademark celebration on 208 occasions!

The common will of the Red Army helped Joe by sucking the ball into the tempting net!

This is a commonplace phenomenon in grounds where the vocal home support is located at one end behind the goal.

In the context of crowds, Pittodrie had the first ever all seated, covered, stadium and that's also where the first dugouts came into vogue. In 1934, the Aberdeen FC trainer, innovative Donald Coleman, had that brainwave which has left an indelible mark on football.

Careful scrutiny of the imagery in this photographic masterpiece will, I predict, leave a similarly indelible mark on your mind.

Craig Brown CBE, 2021.

CONTENTS

The grounds aren't in alphabetical order. This is designed as a dip-in-dip-out book with gems scattered throughout the chapters.

Winning it on corners

WHEN you think about an old football ground, you might try to analyse what it was you liked about it. What was it – exactly – that gave it such character? Why were they so recognisable? What was the idiosyncrasy that instantly identified them as Brockville, Gayfield or Somerset Park?

Was it the shape of the terracing roof? The oddities of the main stand? For me it was the corners, where one terrace met another.

Perhaps this is a notion that has grown as a by-product of my disdain for the modern, one-size-fits-all football stand. Today's grounds rarely get their corners right. They don't join. They have the abrupt end of a stand behind the goal huffily turning a cold shoulder towards the equally soul-less blandstand that runs down the shy line.

They always look slightly uncomfortable, as if the architect ran out of ideas and is hoping no one will notice. They have embarrassing spaces you can see into but where you aren't supposed to look – like a man with his flies down.

In the old days, corners had a little imagination. A flourish of the architect's pencil. They were things of beauty. They looked like they were an intended part of the ground, that had been thought about, planned for, and put in place with pride and skilled workmanship.

The old bowl-shaped grounds, like Hampden, Ibrox, Celtic Park, Rugby Park and several others, didn't even need corners. They had an long, dignified sweep. They were curvy, shapely and highly attractive.

But even the more angular grounds coped with their corners in a more elegant way.

■ **Right: Dens Park's newly-concreted corner at the Provost Road end, pictured in 1962, upon which a builder had worked hard.**

Motherwell hero Charlie Aitken, a one-club man who played 415 games for the Steelmen over 17 seasons, displays his prodigious heading power in a photo that also shows off the well-crafted corner of Fir Park in the early 1960s. This is what a football ground should look like.

■ There's another attractive, curvaceous, indeed quite sexy, corner joining seamlessly and naturally to the side terracing. It is St Mirren's Love Street on August 12th, 1961. A 16,000 crowd saw a Tommy Bryceland goal beat Kilmarnock in a sun-kissed League Cup sectional tie. There was greyhound racing at Love Street in the 1930s, and speedway in the 1970s – both possible thanks to those rounded corners.

14

■ **Above:** the corner between the Beach End and South Side of Pittodrie required skilled joinery to make the bench seats fit together. It was an uncovered area for several years and in part still is (this is a 1978 photo) so the weather rolling in off the North Sea made it uncomfortable at times. But it was still a bonny corner.

■ **Left:** Falkirk's Brockville had a schoolboys' corner – which sometimes overflowed. This pic is from 1963.

■ At Stark's Park, they got round the what-to-do-with-a-corner problem by building a stand on it. This is a Raith Rovers v Aberdeen cup-tie on January 24th, 1981, that The Dons won 2-1. The hemmed-in geography of Stark's Park made the corner placement of the stand the obvious option – it was where there was most space. An L-shaped grandstand was highly innovative for its time. There weren't many like it throughout the football world in 1922.

■ A few miles away in Dunfermline, East End Park also had an L-shaped covered corner (must be a Fife thing!) though this one was above terracing. This is Dunfermline v Celtic, September 6th, 1969, with The Pars' John McGarty in the foreground in what is an all-blue change strip. Alex Edwards and Celtic's Harry Hood are behind him, with Tommy Gemmell further back. It was a 2-1 home win in a great game at a noisy East End Park packed with a 25,000 crowd.

■ Dundee United's Tannadice Park.

After its late-1950s refurbishment, when the pitch was moved several yards to the north, Tannadice had instantly-recognisable triangular corner walls – for many years known as the "Skol Corners" (though they later became "TSB Corners").

The steep, concreted terraces climbed up and around the corner flags like no other stadium. They offered a good view and were always a popular place to stand.

This photo shows the east (Arklay Street) end of the ground and there was another very similar corner at the "Shed" end of the ground.

This is a visiting Rangers crowd waiting for the teams to run out on December 27th, 1975 – policed by a solitary copper.

The crowd of 13,011 saw a 0-0 draw.

■ Grounds with oval tracks didn't have the same corner problems. The terrace followed the line of the terracing wall. This is pre-season training at Celtic Park for the 1967-68 season.

■ There were lovely, crafted corners at Airdrie's Broomfield. Some clever architect or gaffer worked out how the terrace would curve behind the goal and positioned the pavilion to match. This end is probably best described as a half-ellipse, not quite a full semi-circle but certainly not straight either.

■ **No such thing as a corner at Hampden, with that beautiful, long and smooth (though largely empty in this case) curve.**

This is the Scottish Cup Semi-Final of Tuesday, April 6th, 1982 – a famous night in the history of Forfar Athletic FC.

The Loons had held Rangers to a 0-0 draw the previous Saturday, but went down 3-1 in this replay.

Rangers fans sang "There's nae bridies left", which was a tribute (of sorts) to the part-time Angus club.

■ Shawfield, having had a greyhounds track since 1932, always had semi-circular terraces behind the goals.

Another ground where there were no terracing corners, as such, just smooth rounded ends.

Clyde became tenants of the greyhound company, rather than it being the other way around, in 1935.

But Shawfield had always been that shape. Even before Clyde took up residence, in 1898, it had been a trotting track.

This picture shows Clyde's accomplished full-back Harry Haddock giving Aberdeen's Graham Leggat a piece of his mind.

Famously, and to his great credit, Harry was never once booked in a 14-year club and international career.

But he was certainly no pushover.

If there was a fault with Ibrox after the reconstruction of the late-70s/early-80s, it was the yawning corner gaps between the stands. However, Rangers – to the club's credit – realised this and solved the problem in the 1990s by filling the corners with the Struth Stand Club Deck access towers, and seats and electronic scoreboards adjoining the Govan Stand, with the Rangers shop behind. The new "enclosed" feel instantly improved the atmosphere. If only more clubs would find a way to fill their corner gaps!

■ St Johnstone's Muirton (left), and McDiarmid Park (above). The older photo shows a curved corner where fans stood, or walked round as they changed ends at half-time. But Muirton was becoming decrepit, and grassed spectator areas (even with concrete terrace in front) wouldn't be allowed today. The new ground has all the comforts and benefits of a modern stadium and brought many advantages. But it has wide gaps in the corners and movement between stands is not permitted. Each type of corner had its benefits, each has drawbacks. It is up to the individual to decide which type of corner – and which ground – they like best. Perhaps it is acceptable to say you loved the old and still miss it, while also supporting the move to the new?

Hibernian's Easter Road. This is how it should be done – a proper corner, with concreted steps and crush barriers. It takes a craftsman to create this.

Each step in the corner has to be of the correct width to join to its neighbours which face straight on to the side-line and goal-line. As a diagonal cut is always longer than a straight cut, it isn't easy to match them.

The concrete will be poured into wooden boxes and left to set, so the sides of those boxes each must be cut to the specific length required. No two will be the same as they grow longer further up the terrace.

The crush barriers have to be embedded, so their positions must be planned. To complicate matters, not all crush barriers on a corner section will be at the same angle (as the bottom left of this photo shows).

There is the added problem of the walkway. It is set at a lower level so fans won't stand in it (they wouldn't be able to see). It must be straight, though.

The concrete mix must be right: not too much sand, not too much gravel or the step will crumble or flake and require to be patched. Some patching work is visible on this terrace.

It is imperative that new concrete is left long enough to "cure". This is a chemical process in which cement forms crystals at a microscopic level which bind strongly to each other. Badly-cured concrete will crack.

To aid the curing process it is best if, after being poured, the concrete is kept covered by plastic or canvas and remains slightly damp for several days.

Constructing a proper stadium corner was a complicated business, but aesthetically very pleasing. And – importantly – a good corner allowed more paying spectators in.

Rangers

THE main stand, now the Struth Stand, at Ibrox is the most magnificent example of classic football architecture still standing in the world. We are lucky to have it in Scotland and more should be made of it.

Ibrox is the greatest, and last, example of the work of the celebrated Archibald Leitch, the man who designed almost all of the grandest grandstands in Britain during the first three decades of the last century. He built Hampden, Old Trafford, Villa Park, Goodison Park, White Hart Lane and Highbury, among dozens more.

But Ibrox was his biggest project and remains his crowning achievement.

The South Stand was completed in 1928 and had 10,500 seats, with an enclosure in front.

In all it cost £95,000 – more than any club in Britain had ever paid to build a single stand.

Leitch had previously won acclaim for his work at Villa Park, and the outside of the Ibrox stand was constructed of the same material, red Welsh brick. But where the Villa Park stand was ornate, the stand at Ibrox was a much more restrained design.

It wasn't intended to look frivolous, there was a very different intention (see next page).

■ **Willie Waddell, a giant himself in the story of Ibrox, with the main stand as a magnificent backdrop.**

It is impossible to fully appreciate or understand that Ibrox main stand without taking into account the beliefs, personality and ambition of Bill Struth.

Mr Struth joined Rangers as trainer in 1914 and became manager on May 20th, 1920. He remained in-post until June 15th, 1954, a full 34 years. He imposed standards of behaviour and dress on his players that were intended to mark them as "Rangers men".

He would insist the entire team wore the turns on their socks to the same depth, that they rolled up their sleeves to a uniform length, and that they didn't put on their shorts until just before they took to the field in case they became creased.

Off the field, they wore made-to-measure suits, bowler hats and round toe-capped shoes shined well, and would march rather than walk. The intention was to impress and intimidate any opposition. And it worked. Rangers were incredibly successful during his reign.

Bill Struth wanted his club to be the best and show that they were the best. It is an ambition that to this day lies at the heart of how Rangers supporters, and the club, see themselves.

And his football ground was constructed with the same aim.

A magnificent building speaks of the power and potency of its owners – indeed many buildings are designed to do solely that.

In football, however, the usual measure of a club's stature is its tally of trophies.

But if you can have both, the impressive surroundings and the on-field success, then none can deny your standing in the game.

Any who walk into Ibrox (Rangers supporter or not) will be impressed – perhaps even awed – by the surroundings.

■ **Left: Mr Struth in front of the grandstand that now bears his name. He died on September 21st, 1956, but his influence is still felt – and can still plainly be seen by all who visit Ibrox – to this day.**

Mr Struth consulted at length with Leitch on how the main stand should look, because the look was important.

The symmetrical outside brickwork has pilasters (depictions of classical columns) along the front, reminiscent of ancient Greek architecture.

The two-storey windows have semi-circular arches like cathedral windows.

At each end of the structure tower-like blocks have pointed pediments above the windows – like the Parthenon in Athens.

The surrounds and window at the main entrance are constructed to look like the barbican of a castle.

It is a cherry-picked mixture of architectural styles (as many grand but functional buildings are) but works very well. The stand was intended to denote sturdiness, longevity, dignity and power. It fulfils all those aims.

It is a statement building.

■ **This photo shows the main stand in 1989, before the Club Deck was added.**

■ This is October 1981. The new Ibrox. The addition of the Club Deck would result in the pillars being removed from the front of the main stand. It also gave a height symmetry on all four sides as the Leitch stand, the prime statement building, couldn't be left even slightly dwarfed by its surroundings.

39

If anything, the addition of the upper deck only added to the grandeur of the Struth Stand.

The creation of the corporate Club Deck took the experience of attending a football match at Ibrox (if you'll forgive the pun) to a new level. These facilities are an essential part of the modern game.

The project was initially to cost £14 million, but the final bill was more than £20 million.

The street-side frontage of Ibrox is a B-listed building and cannot be altered (not that there was any desire to change the traditional look) but it did present construction difficulties.

New foundations, beneath the existing founds, had to be inserted, and the main steel truss holding up the roof and top deck was the biggest ever created anywhere in the world. It required the two biggest cranes ever built to hoist it into place.

The result is impressive. A meld of old and new that, importantly, remains aesthetically pleasing and ensures the stadium stays true to its history. The stand now holds 20,370 – 5,267 seats on the former enclosure, 7,820 on the main deck, and 7,283 in the upper deck.

The Struth Stand has been the most impressive, and historically significant, football building in Britain for more than nine decades – and it still is.

■ May 8th, 1993. Rangers 1, Dundee United 0. Rangers were presented with the Premiership trophy after the last home game of the season. This was the mid-point of the club's nine-in-a-row run of championships. The stand enclosure was still a standing area at this point.

■ One of the design differences that separates the Struth Stand from most other stands at Scottish grounds is that it was created as an administration/offices block, with a stand at its front – rather than being a stand, with sloped-ceiling rooms tucked below the seating area. The stand faces the pitch, the offices face Edmiston Drive – as illustrated in this 1937 photo.

■ The Ibrox stand enclosure is an example of how changing safety regulations affected capacities.

When the enclosure opened in 1928 it was to hold a precise 15,496.

Leitch's calculation was (for all his grounds) to allow each spectator an area of one terrace step 16 inches wide. If you add up the length of every terrace step – all round the ground – and divide by 16 inches, then add the number of grandstand seats, you are left with a total that is a stadium's notional capacity.

During the 1930s, '40s and '50s, when Ibrox held up to 118,000, over 17,000 were squeezed in to the stand enclosure.

In the 1977 plan for the revamp of Ibrox, the enclosure capacity was set at 9,000. At that point, it was stated the enclosure would be retained in perpetuity to provide a choice for those who still wanted to watch football on their feet.

That didn't last, though. The final standing capacity, just before the 1990s rebuild of the stand, was 7,500.

Yet through the years it barely changed – same footprint, same number of steps, same crush barriers.

■ **East Fife outside-right Jackie Stewart takes a corner in front of the covered terrace on the Govan (north) side.**

Ibrox had suffered a disaster in 1902, when wooden plank terracing erected on scaffolding collapsed during a Scotland v England game.

Vowing that this would never happen again, the Rangers board had the ground rebuilt as a vast bowl with earth banks.

A rail line was being constructed right behind the north terracing so Rangers secured the earth and rubble dug out of the cutting to build up the slopes for the three standing sides of the ground.

As luck would have it, when the terraces were being replaced by stands in the early 1980s, the track had become surplus to the rail network's needs, so all the earth went back where it came from.

The Derry had this distinctive barrel roof until 1954 (see also next page) but then had a double-pitched angular roof built. But if you looked up you could still see the original structure.

It had bench seats installed in 1973 and became known as the Centenary Stand, though many a Rangers man was sorry to see the loudest, most partisan stance of the Ibrox "choir" made into a seated area.

■ The terracing roof in 1935. This was Ibrox in its peak capacity years. Archie Leitch had used his capacity-calculating equation (see page 43) to declare that this, the zenith of his career in stadium design, allowed crowds of more than 100,000. From 1929 until the 1970s this was the second highest capacity ground in Britain (behind only Hampden).

■ Left: Davie Wilson at the Broomloan End in 1963. Above: Winger George Duncan, who didn't have a long Ibrox career, in 1957. The two photos give us a good view of the terraces. Those vast standing areas allowed record-setting crowds, but meant some spectators were a long way from the action. The stated aim when new stands were being planned was to ensure no seat would be more than 90 metres from the centre circle.

This is why it had to change – indeed why all football grounds had to change. This is the notorious Stairway 13 where the Ibrox Disaster of 1971 happened.

You will find tens of thousands of people in Scotland (all of them over the age of 50) who will have been to one of our bigger football stadiums in the days when massive crowds were packed in.

Some will talk of being worried and frightened, and tell of being so tightly squeezed when moving toward the exit gates that they could lift their feet off the ground and be carried forward. But just as many will say that it was exciting and perhaps even comforting, or that it gave a sense of camaraderie, to be part of a seething crowd all wanting the same thing – a win for their team.

The most puzzling question is not why accidents happened in these huge crowds – it was inevitable that a trip, a stumble, would cause an accident one day.

The real question is: why didn't an awful lot more accidents happen?

The assumption, of those who never felt what it was like being in those crowds, is of an uncaring mass who would trample and push. But tens of thousands making their way out of a football ground expected there would be a crush (there was a crush every week).

They patiently moved at the pace of those around them, sure in the knowledge that once past the choke-point of the exit gates, or bottom of a stairway, the crowd would thin and people would go on their way. No problem, no harm done.

There has been huge strides in the science of crowd management since the 1970s. If you were ever part of a giant crowd, and read the conclusions of those studies, you'll recognise what they are talking about. Not because scientists and computer modellers worked it out, but because you lived it.

There were unwritten rules. You didn't push, and you didn't try go against the flow. You went with those around you, and did it calmly. Older men looked after youngsters, who would sometimes be lifted out of danger. If you saw someone stumble, you'd grab their arm to keep them upright.

Only a panicking crowd pushes, or tramples, or falls upon those around them because they have tripped (as happened on Stairway 13 in 1971). Those who went to football in the 1950s, '60s and '70s didn't panic. They were vastly experienced at dealing with being shoulder-to-shoulder in a tight-packed crowd.

■ **This is September 1969, Willie Wallace (Celtic) and Ron MacKinnon (Rangers) up for a high ball. The crowd was a mere 75,000.**

The one thing a photo cannot do is portray what the noise would be like when a crowd like this was gathered.

The atmosphere inside Ibrox this day would have been an almost physical force.

The biggest ever attendance was on January 2nd, 1939, when 118,567 were in the ground for a 2-1 New Year win over the old rivals.

It was a world record for a league game.

Ibrox would record six-figure gates three more times before the 1971 Ibrox Disaster changed everything.

The profits of Rangers Pools are what paid for the re-build of Ibrox.

Rangers weren't the first Scottish club to set up their own football pool operation, but they were by far the most successful.

The pool started in 1964, and at one point in the 1970s, Rangers Pools had 1.3 million lines entered each week and would give jackpots of £30,000 for a bob's stake (£30k in 1970 is the equivalent of £475,000 today – a "bob" was 5p).

There were strict tax laws governing what the money could be used for. Development of the ground was allowed, whereas income tax (on top of the 33.3% betting duty) would have had to be paid if the profits were spent on buying or paying players.

The driving force behind Rangers Pools was Ibrox director Davie Hope, who deserves a high rank in the list of Rangers heroes.

He recruited an army of agents who would give out, then go back to collect, coupons in their workplace, or pub, or round the doors. These agents made their way to Ibrox, or handed over their takings to someone who would, to deliver their cash.

Many, many more people took part than just those who were Rangers supporters. It became commonplace to see smiling, very respectable ladies in their Sunday best, who often had no interest in

■ **Bobby Watson presents a lucky winner with her cheque before the Rangers v Hearts game of January 11th, 1969. Rangers won 2-0.**

■ **A 1970 article from *The Weekly News* predicting the great things all that pools money would do for Ibrox in the coming decade.**

football and might never have been inside a ground in their life, invited to Ibrox to be presented with their cheques by players or directors, or sometimes high and mighty general manager Willie Waddell himself.

All those agents bringing in a couple of quid, all those respectable ladies – and the hard work of Davie Hope organising all this – week after week, season after season, added up to the huge Govan, Copland Road and Broomloan stands.

Archie Leitch registered his "crush rails", as they were described, with the Patent Office in 1906.

They had tubular steel bars on top of tightly curved stanchions (formed from one piece of steel) both ends firmly embedded in the concrete. Then there was a strengthening bar at an angle below the corners, pointing back along the length.

They were remarkably strong.

The classic Leitch crush barriers at the Copland Road End of Ibrox are visible behind John Prentice (with Alex Scott watching) doing heading practice.

Other grounds throughout Scotland had similar constructions, although many were of the less safe single-stanchion design. Some were made of wood.

The Leitch barriers proved extremely durable, staying unmoved despite exposure to decade after decade of Scotland's rust-inducing weather punctuated every few weeks by the pressures of tight-packed crowds.

These barriers were almost universally installed in the stadiums Leitch designed and many remained in place for 80 years, until the Taylor Report of 1990 swept away terraces altogether.

Indeed, only one of the Leitch barriers at Sheffield Wednesday's Hillsborough collapsed in the lethal crush of the terrible 1989 disaster, despite having been in place for three-quarters of a century.

However, strong barriers or not, terraces were doomed from that day. These barriers had been designed as a safety measure but eventually were deemed to have become part of the problem.

The Rangers barriers were, of course, removed in the 1970s rebuild of Ibrox.

■ This photo was taken to show off the new sectional anti-frost pitch guard at Ibrox in 1969 (see Weather chapter in Volume 3) but serves to illustrate just how vast the curved Copland Road End was in those days. It should be compared to the photo on the next page.

■ This photo was taken in 1981, soon after the Copland Road Stand opened. It is from a slightly lower angle than the previous page, but the two photos illustrate the extent of the Ibrox transformation.

Clyde

SHAWFIELD was the stadium that went to the dogs. It's a terrible pun, and was a terrible shame.

The "Old Firm" could have been a three-way association, with Clyde as the third force. The potential for the club was as big as for any in the land when football was snowballing in popularity in the late 19th and early 20th Centuries. A 100,000 capacity was Shawfield's original aim.

Clyde were a big draw in those early years. Of all the clubs talked of on these pages, Clyde's highest crowd is the only one that is pre-World War 1.

But things went wrong. Clyde found themselves in need of money between the wars and the answer looked like it might have four legs. A new attraction was sweeping the land – greyhound racing. It was a long-odds chance to bet your way out of poverty.

The Shawfield lease didn't allow animal racing (cheetah racing was also staged in Scotland at the time) so the club directors set up an independent greyhound company, and it bought the ground in 1935.

This worked quite well for years, with football and greyhounds sharing the stadium.

In 1971 the Greyhound Racing Association bought Shawfield. The football tenants were then always secondary to this national organisation's priorities. After the dogs operation began to record losses the GRA put the ground up for sale in 1984 and Clyde were given 18 months' notice to leave.

They moved out in 1986 and suffered a hard existence as lodgers at Firhill and Douglas Park for eight years until moving to a new home at Broadwood in Cumbernauld, 15 miles from Shawfield.

Shawfield never actually was developed as housing, or a retail park (as per the sale plan) and reopened as a race track in 1987.

The biggest crowd at the old stadium is a matter of dispute, possibly a matter of fiction!

It is usually cited as either 52,000 against Rangers in November 1908, or 46,500 against Celtic in 1912. It is entirely possible, though, that neither of these figures is correct. No one really knows.

Shawfield had a bad safety record and suffered a disaster in 1957. A crowd of 31,000 were at a League match against Celtic on December 14th. As was normal in big attendances, children sat on the track.

However, when Celtic scored an early goal a crowd surge pushed over the perimeter wall, injuring 50 people, 13 of them seriously. Nine-year-old James Ryan died with a crushed chest cavity.

■ **Right: Shawfield's magnificent Art Deco gates pictured just before the Second World War.**

■ **Above:** The crowd at Shawfield had to watch from a distance, with the dog track between them and the pitch. However, the facilities were quite advanced. The ground had, relatively early by Scottish standards, properly concreted terracing, a well-appointed stand, and plenty cover. This picture shows Dundee's Jim Watt warming up in 1956 with Shawfield's covered enclosure behind. It is a wet day with the supporters – a lot of demob overcoats on show here – huddled together out of the rain.

■ **Right:** In a slightly light-damaged photo, Rangers' George Young takes a corner in 1954. Despite the dog track, there was room for corners to be taken at Shawfield – this certainly wasn't the case at all grounds with race-tracks. Often the corners were cut into by the racing lanes.

■ Shawfield's pitch was in a dip slightly below the level of the dog track and the surrounding terraces. It flooded easily and often, and the goalmouths especially would become gluepots. The above photo is Alex Bryce scoring Clyde's goal against Celtic on New Year's Day 1966, a 3-1 win for the visitors on a wet, muddy afternoon. The south end of the ground was dominated by the giant tote board and the social club,

restaurant and betting booths (these buildings can be seen in these photos). The tote board was built in the 1930s and remained until 2004, long after Clyde had moved away. The photo on this page, which gives a good view of the social club, shows Clyde's renowned Scotland international striker Tommy Ring trying a shot v Rangers on November 15th, 1952 – a rip-snorting 6-4 away win in front of 28,000.

■ Willie Steel doing keepie-ups at training in 1960, in a pic illustrating the height difference between dog track and pitch.

■ Harry Haddock also doing keepie-ups, in a pic showing the nicely paved stand enclosure.

■ The Lanarkshire/City of Glasgow border passed right through the stadium. During the war, big crowds weren't supposed to gather for fear of bombing raids – as the people of Clydebank, just a few miles away from Shawfield, well knew. However, the regulations weren't consistent. Shawfield was (mostly) outwith the Glasgow City boundary so Clyde (in Lanarkshire) were allowed crowds up to 20,000 while Celtic Park, less than a mile away but deemed to be in a major city, was officially limited to 10,000. However, these guidelines must have been ignored by the clubs as Celtic regularly recorded big crowds in the war years.

■ Clyde's later problems attracting crowds can be directly attributed to the demolition of the heavily-populated housing areas that used to be close to Shawfield.

The post-war slum clearances, that reached their peak in the 1960s, resulted in greatly reduced populations in Rutherglen, Bridgeton, Dalmarnock, Gorbals and Oatlands. The Clyde heartlands.

It was progress, but not for the club's turnstile clicks.

The native support was rehoused out to the new towns or stacked high in multi-storey flats – and they never came back.

This photo shows Clyde legend Harry Haddock again (it's rare to find an old Clyde photo without Harry in it!) running towards Shawfield through the tenement-lined streets that used to be the home territory of the Bully Wee crowds.

■ **There were few terraces anywhere in British football that stretched so far under one unbroken roof as Shawfield's long, curved shed.**

This photo shows the shed in 1951, behind Clyde goalie Charlie Thomson, before his transfer to Chelsea.

Charlie would win a league title with the London club, then an FA Cup winners' medal with Nottingham Forest.

■ A glimpse behind the Shawfield scenes. Clyde's players before a 4-1 victory over Hamilton Accies in April 1966. Manager was the young Davie White (in the suit) who had just steered Clyde to their best league position in years. It was unusual to allow cameras into any club's dressing room in those days, but White had new and fresh ideas about football management and would be poached by Rangers to replace Scot Symon.

■ **A glorious day. April 26th, 1958.**

Greeted by raucous cheers Clyde captain Harry Haddock dangles the Scottish Cup precariously out of the Shawfield Stadium window.

The Bully Wee beat Hibs 1-0 to win the Cup for the third (and so far last) time.

They made the short trip back to their own ground for a celebration party.

Clyde had done something no other club in the world has ever matched. They won their national Cup in 1955, were relegated in '56, won promotion in '57, and won the Cup again in '58.

What a four years!

Aberdeen

THE conversion of Pittodrie into an all-seater arena is remarkable not just because it was done before most clubs even considered it, but because it was managed without going into debt and with the enthusiasm of the club's supporters.

This photo shows Pittodrie with its pavilion in the Beach End/Main Stand corner during an Aberdeen-Rangers game on September 7th, 1929. It was a 1-1 draw in front of 32,600 spectators.

Over the years, great change would come.

Pittodrie's biggest ever crowd, 45,061, rolled up on March 13th, 1954, for a Scottish Cup Quarter-Final against Hearts. It was an all-ticket game, with 8,000 briefs sent to Edinburgh. Every ticket, in both the capital and Aberdeen, was snapped up.

Football was booming in the north, with Dave Halliday's multi-talented side looking like they would seriously challenge for honours.

Hearts were also doing well, armed with their Terrible Trio, Alfie Conn, Willie Bauld and Jimmy Wardhaugh. They were top of the league, Aberdeen were third.

Indeed, the hard-pressed staff at Aberdeen FC reckoned they could have sold many more tickets for this game, with estimates claiming up to 60,000 would have been inside Pittodrie if there had been room.

Early in the cup-tie, Hearts' Bobby Parker, who would go on to become chairman of the Edinburgh club, was involved in an ugly retaliation incident with Aberdeen's English winger Jack Hather. It wasn't seen by the ref but Parker was deafeningly booed by the home support for the rest of the game.

Hearts wore an unfamiliar white strip and were handed a 3-1 beating. The Dons' scorers were Joe O'Neil, Graham Leggat and George Hamilton.

Aberdeen would meet Rangers in the semi-final – one of the most famous games in the club's history up to then, a 6-0 win at Hampden in front of 110,939.

Pittodrie has been continually altered and improved over the years.

The Paddock got its roof in 1934, though the Beach End wasn't covered until the summer of 1958. The floodlight pylons were put up in 1959.

The ornamental gates at the Merkland Road End went up in 1928, built in traditional Aberdeen granite hewn from Rubislaw Quarry, the same rock much of the rest of the city is constructed from.

The corner stand, between the main stand and Beach End, that always seemed to face slightly the wrong way, was built in 1937 to replace the pavilion that can be seen on the first page of this chapter.

	COVERED TERRACING	SEATED
GRAND STAND		4,200
DIRECTORS & PRESS		78
ENCLOSURE	4500	
		4278
TOTAL COVERED		8778
WEST BANK	14202	
EAST BANK	15720	
SOUTH BANK	12000	
TOTAL		50,700

■ **Could Pittodrie have ever held 60,000? Not according to the Archie Leitch plans for the ground discovered by the detective work of Ms Sue Shepherd in the Old Aberdeen Archives. The capacity was to be 50,700, as shown by Leitch's 1920s calculations.**

■ The incident between Hearts' Bobby Parker (No. 2) and Jack Hather mentioned on the opposite page.

The crowded terraces behind the Beach End goal can just be made out in the background.

Pittodrie in the early 1950s.

Aberdeen legend Fred Martin in front of the old Paddock in 1954.

■ August 1968, the main stand's enclosure in the process of being built up to become an extension of the stand's seated area, pitched at the same angle. The roof was also re-configured to cover all the seats. This work brought the stand's capacity up to 6,000 from its original 4,278.

■ **The extent of the huge south terracing is apparent in this 1975 photo, and the earlier photo on the opposite page. At the time of the above photo, Pittodrie's capacity was still around 45,000.**

■ Aberdeen v Celtic Scottish Cup Quarter-Final, March 9th, 1935. The crowd was 40,105. Aberdeen won 3-1.

Several times in these books the practice of children sitting on the cinder track has been mentioned. This photo gives a good view of it happening.

In dense crowds children would be passed down over the heads and deposited on the track. It is an example of the easy, almost second-nature, habits of practicality and team-work that men (many of whom had served in the Army) seemed to possess in those days.

The children would stay on the track, their father or older brothers waiting until the crowd thinned at the end of the game and then collecting them.

A few got lost for a wee while, or fretted because they couldn't see their dad, but it always worked out in the end.

However, this arrangement depended on impeccable behaviour from the boys at pitch-side. They had to sit and watch the game going on just a few feet away.

When that type of disciplined behaviour broke down in society, the clubs and police could no longer allow spectators within touching distance of footballers.

■ **Left: The Beach End gets bench seats in 1973, whereas (above) The Paddock had seats installed in 1971 (though this photo was taken in 1985 showing the new roof).**

There is often debate over whether Clydebank's New Kilbowie or Pittodrie was the first all-seater stadium in the UK.

Technically, it was Kilbowie in 1977, although there are particular circumstances. At the time, clubs had to comply with the Safety of Sports Grounds Act, but only if they had a capacity above 10,000.

Clydebank bolted bench seats to their unroofed terracing to reduce capacity to 9,950 – thereby avoiding having to make further expensive alterations.

Pittodrie was all-seated by 1978, and got a roof on the South Side in 1980 (see next page), making it the first planned and proper all-seater ground in Britain with cover over (almost) all of its seated sections.

■ Pittodrie in 1979.

■ In January 1980 Aberdeen chairman Dick Donald and vice-chairman Chris Anderson unveiled their plans to cover all sides of Pittodrie. Then (unlike some other clubs who publish ambitious plans and then do very little – a common occurrence over the years throughout Scottish football) quickly got to work to make those plans a reality. By July 27th, 1980 (above), the steel was in place for the South Stand roof. The bench seats didn't last long, however, they were soon replaced by tip-ups

■ **The Richard Donald Stand takes shape in 1993. There is an illustration here of the effect changing health & safety rules have had on the capacity of even an all-seater ground. When Pittodrie was first made all-seated in 1978, capacity was given as 24,000. The replacement of bench seats with individual seats brought it down to 22,568. But despite the opening of this huge, modern stand the ground's capacity is now 20,866.**

■ The main stand at Pittodrie suffered a spectacular fire in the early hours of Saturday, February 6th, 1971. Historical artefacts from the club's early days, were lost, including many details of the Archie Leitch design for the stadium. The Dons were holders of the Scottish Cup at the time, but firefighters with breathing apparatus felt their way through to the smoke-filled trophy room to rescue the cup and pass it out a window.

■ Right: Three months later, the rebuild is in full swing. To this day there is still a difference in the stand roof which shows the fire-hit rebuilt section and the older section.

Dugouts

THE football stadium dugout was conceived in the 1930s by Aberdeen trainer Donald Colman to get closer to his players. It was good idea. Soon every stadium had them.

This simple start began with simple constructions, and grew.

And dugouts took on a new role. They became a side stage to the main stage. The agony and ecstasy the fans feel is mirrored, perhaps magnified, in those hut-like constructions.

If there was drama on the pitch, there was often more drama in the dugout – wild celebrations, incandescent anger, laughs and jokes, or the stony stoicism of a manager who knows events have conspired against him to the point where he is about to lose his job.

Some dugouts were a long way from the tunnel. Many a manager (see Craig Brown's introduction) dreaded running the gauntlet past fans.

Of course, as with everything else about Scottish stadiums, no two had dugouts of the same build, height, width, layout, or number of seats.

But many had character to match the characters who sat in them.

■ **George Young, on his first day as Third Lanark manager in 1959, in the Cathkin Park dugout. It was one of the below-ground-level types (quite common in Scotland) and gave a very limited view of what was happening on the pitch.**

■ Jim McLean's volcanic eruptions from his Tannadice dugout were legendary. This is Dundee United v Aberdeen on August 31, 1991. A 0-0 draw. Note the padded roof edges to stop hot heads being bumped.

■ **Rangers coach Joe Mason (a former Killie, Morton and Rangers player) lights up a cigarette in the Ibrox dugout. It looks odd in these post-smoking days but was normal in 1978. Rangers are playing Hearts (and winning 3-1) in the short-lived Tennent-Caledonian Cup, a pre-season tournament involving Rangers and Hearts along with West Brom and Southampton from down south. It was staged four times at Ibrox between 1976 and 1979 with Rangers inviting different guests each season.**

■ Above: dugouts, positioned one on each side of the players' tunnel, was a popular layout at grounds. This is Muirton Park, former home of St Johnstone. The directors' box, a small area of the centre stand separated from the rest of the crowd by a low wooden partition, was another common feature of the Scottish football stand. It allowed disgruntled punters easy access to inform directors that they were overweight chaps, born out of wedlock, who needed to put their hands deeper into their pockets and buy a new centre-forward as the current one wasn't quite up to scratch.

■ The Muirton Park dugouts again, on April 18th, 1976. Dundee boss Davie White (middle) and coaches George Blues (left) and Hugh Robertson contort in agony as St Johnstone equalise through former Dens Park defender Ian Anderson. This fourth last game of the season ended as a 1-1 draw, the Perth men winning only their eighth point of the season. Dundee were relegated – on goal-difference – and Davie lost his job the following year.

■ The Celtic Park dugouts in 1974. Athletico Madrid boss Juan Carlos Lorenzo (the same man who managed Argentina in 1966 – the team England boss Alf Ramsey labelled "animals") tells our photographer exactly what he thinks of the ref's decision to dismiss Ruben Ayala in the European Cup Semi-Final First Leg. Ayala had been sent off in what was one of the most brutal games ever played in Scotland, but refused to go any further than the away dugout. The placement of Mr Lorenzo's right hand may, or may not, be significant in an explanation of his feelings towards Turkish ref Dogan Babacan, the evening's game, or life in general.

■ The thing about dugouts is that though they are a place for managers to sit, they do tend to get out of them often. Alex Ferguson salutes Dom Sullivan's equaliser during his first visit to Ibrox as Aberdeen boss on September 16th, 1978. It was an important part of Ferguson's strategy to not be, or even appear to be, overawed when his Dons team played in Glasgow. Fergie celebrated goals and victories as if he owned the place, caring not one whit for the enclosure full of disgruntled Rangers supporters close behind him.

■ Keeping Jock Wallace enclosed was never easy either. This is November 19th, 1983. The first home game of his second spell as Rangers manager. Jock salutes the Copland Road Stand chanting his name. Legend has it that Ibrox had a dugout heating system installed in the 1970s – but only the home dugout.

■ A picture says a thousand words . . . most of them unprintable. A dugout can be a lonely place, no matter how many people are sitting in it. This is Dens Park, Dundee v Alloa Athletic, on January 14th, 1978. Wasps boss Hugh Wilson has just watched Dundee's Billy Pirie score his fourth in a 6-0 rout. Alloa had won promotion the previous season, though they were relegated after just a year in Division 1. But Hugh stayed on as manager until 1980.

■ You will find some reference books which list Antarctica as the coldest place on Earth. This is not true. The coldest place on the planet is Arbroath's Gayfield Park when a biting winter wind is slinging salt sea spray from a high tide across the pitch. Lichties subs Billy Gavine and Alan McKenzie zip up their sleeping bags and get ready to enjoy the delights of a 1-1 draw with Queen of the South on December 6th, 1977.

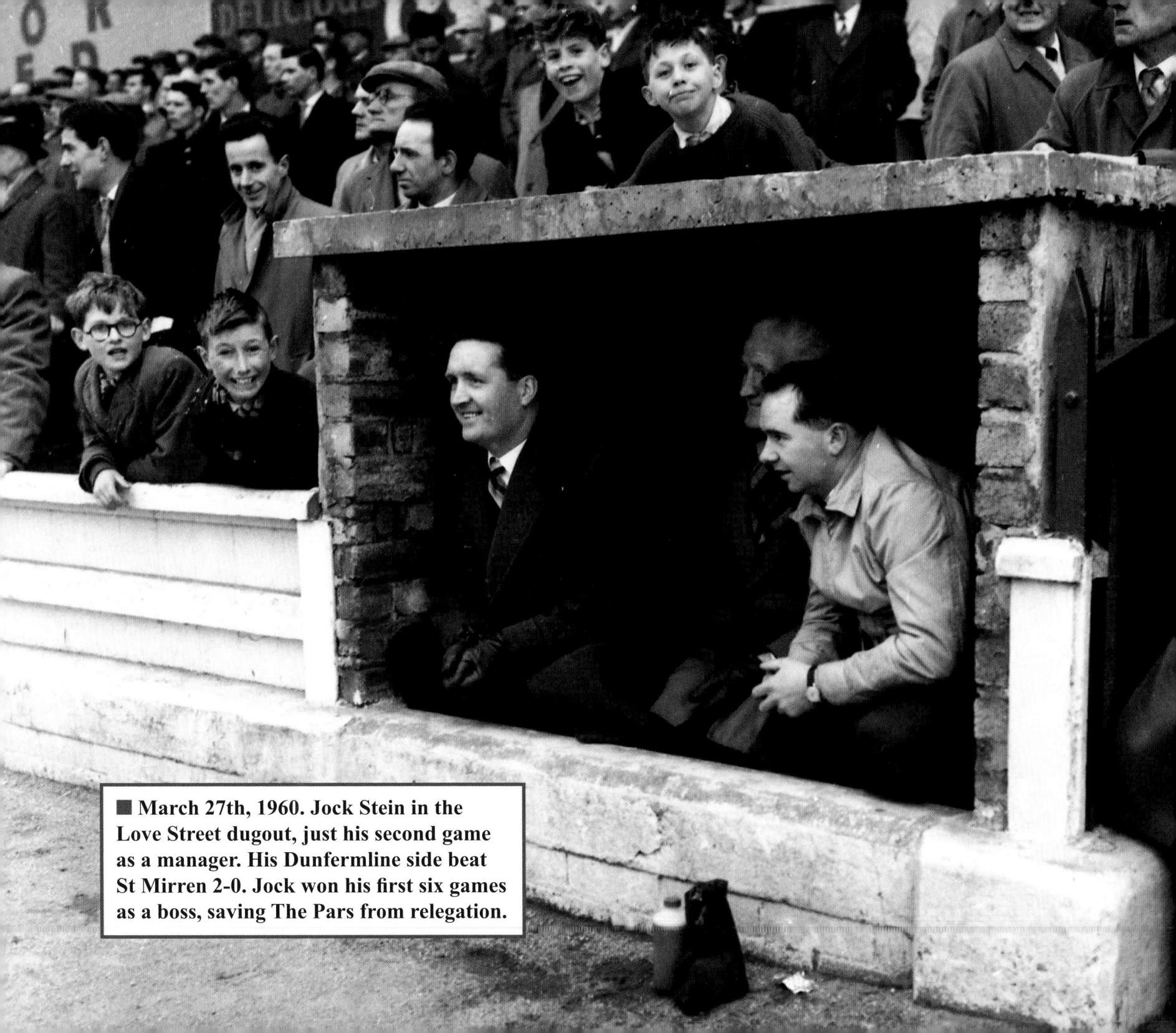

■ **March 27th, 1960. Jock Stein in the Love Street dugout, just his second game as a manager. His Dunfermline side beat St Mirren 2-0. Jock won his first six games as a boss, saving The Pars from relegation.**

Falkirk's Vic McKinney does gymnastics over a Brockville dugout in 1966.

■ Tynecastle's dugouts in the 1960s looked like little camping cabins, and were mostly below pitch level which led many managers to sit outside for a better view. This was March 5th, 1966, a game worth getting a good look at. Sean Fallon points something out to Jock Stein as Celtic draw 3-3 with Hearts in a pulsating Scottish Cup Third Round tie that attracted a crowd officially given as 45,965 but probably much higher.

■ **Celtic v Hearts again, a league encounter later the same year, August 27th, 1966, at Celtic Park. This was the beginning of Celtic's all-conquering season and they won this game 3-0. The dugouts at Celtic underwent many changes over the years, but Jock liked to be out in the open as much as possible.**

■ Andy Paton, voted Motherwell's greatest-ever player, went on to be a long-serving (1959-68) Hamilton Accies manager. This is him in the Douglas Park dugout in 1965.

■ **Dunfermline's East End Park. March 14th, 1970 – referee Archie Walker issues a behaviour warning during a Dunfermline v Rangers game that was "Girvan Lighthouse" Peter McCloy's debut for the away team. The Pars won this ill-tempered encounter 2-1.**

■ **Left: February 6th, 1982. Partick Thistle v St Mirren.**

Dugouts were useless as hiding places when you'd loudly informed the ref that he must be blind and that his big pudden heid deserved to be biled.

This was a feisty 0-0 draw, with Saints' Billy Abercromby sent off in the first half.

But then Billy was used to that sort of thing.

■ **Right: Willie Waddell in his time as Kilmarnock manager in the Rugby Park dugout.**

This is the 1964-65 season, when Deedle had put together the best team in Scotland and was on the way to winning the League title.

■ There were dugouts at Airdrie's Broomfield further along, tucked under the stand. But there was very little room in them. One of the reasons Airdrie had to move was that the pitch was a narrow 67 yards (the bigger Scottish grounds were around 75 yards). Even then, the playing surface was perilously close to the wall of the stand for anyone running full-tilt towards it. These benches for managers and substitutes had the punters almost on top of them. This is a Rangers visit in August 1980, with a newly re-signed Willie Johnston.

■ **One of the great post-war Scottish managers, Bobby Ancell, pictured at his Fir Park dugout in 1965.**

Bobby had a genius for finding talented youngsters and playing them in a way that used their individual talents to the team's best advantage.

He built his Motherwell "Ancell Babes" into a side that couldn't help but entertain.

He was 'Well boss from 1955 to 65 and also managed Dunfermline, Dundee and Berwick.

■ **Rikky McFarlane chose the Love Street dugout (enlarged since the 1960 photo on page 104) to celebrate bringing in Tony Fitzpatrick (re-signed from Bristol City) and Ian Scanlon (from Aberdeen) in May 1981. Helped by these signings, Rikky (uniquely, St Mirren's physio at the same time he was manager) achieved successive 5th-place finishes in 1981-82 and '82-83, but resigned in October 1983.**

■ **September 13th, 1969. This is Ayr v Rangers on the day Somerset Park recorded its biggest ever crowd (see Ayr United chapter in Volume 3). There was no room on the terraces, so some youngsters found an inviting empty bench and sat down . . . only to be surprised when a bloke came along and declared he had a prior booking. Rangers trainer Davie Kinnear is followed down the tunnel by manager Davie White.**

Hampden

O F all the things Scotland is famous for, all the inventions Scots have given the world, all the great men and women who have brought fame to our small country, Hampden Park is rarely included as one of the nation's stellar achievements.

Yet that behemoth of a stadium in Glasgow was for 50 years the greatest on the planet, and can to this day boast attendance figures unmatched anywhere in the northern hemisphere.

Don't trouble yourself to go looking for international or UK domestic club or European crowd records, they are all held by Hampden.

It is the mightiest cathedral of sport that was ever constructed in Europe, Asia or North America.

More so than in any other stadium, going to a big match at Hampden was an all-encompassing experience. It is a shame that younger football fans never experienced, and never will, what it was like to see, hear, and feel what it was like to be among a crowd of 130,000 or 140,000 crammed upon those shallow slopes.

There are a couple of photos on the following pages of the England squad having a walk round the stadium on April 1st, 1966, in preparation for the Scotland-England Home International the next day. Their conversation will have covered an important matter (see next page).

■ **Right: Scotland v. England, April 4th, 1908. At this point it had two south stands, with a pavilion between them. From the moment it opened Hampden drew huge crowds. The attendance at this game was 121,452. Your grandfather or great-grandfather is probably somewhere in this photo.**

The chat, between the experienced and less experienced England players, would have been (as footballers must discuss) the size of the pitch, the studs to wear, the turf, the effect of the wind that sometimes swirled round the ground.

But most of all, the auld heids would be pointing out the difference between an echoing, empty Hampden compared to what it would become the following afternoon, the terraces boiling with Scotsmen urging those in dark blue to superhuman efforts and baying for any man in a white shirt to be eviscerated.

It was an important part of the game that had to be taken into account. The crowd for that game would be 123,052.

The England lads, who would become world champions a few months later, obviously benefitted from this acclimatisation visit as they won 4-3.

■ **Left: Alf Ramsey talks to Alan Ball, who had never played at Hampden before.**

■ **Right: Some of the great names in English football history. From left: Keith Newton, Bobby Moore, Bobby Charlton, Jackie Charlton, Nobby Stiles, Norman Hunter, Roger Hunt and Geoff Hurst.**

■ Hampden Park in 1960. Before the floodlights were erected. It was a giant. A stadium like no other. At its peak in 1937 the notional capacity was 183,388.

■ Hampden's front door, when what is now the car park was used as a football pitch. There are steps up to the modern main entrance, but the car park is largely at the same level as shown here. It was the door that went up.

124

There are few left alive who were inside Hampden for the biggest crowds it ever held. On April 17th, 1937, an attendance of 149,415 saw the Scotland v England game. That is the national team's record.

Seven days later, on April 24th, 1937, the Scottish Cup Final between Celtic and Aberdeen drew in 147,365, setting the club record.

The Scotland v England game of 1939 drew in 149,269 – just 146 fewer than the 1937 game.

To this day, these remain the crowd records for football games in Europe.

Hampden hosted crowds of more than 100,000 on 92 separate occasions.

■ **Left and right: Celtic v Aberdeen, the Scottish Cup Final of 1937 with that 147,365 crowd.**

■ Celtic v Leeds at Hampden in the 1970 European Cup Semi-Final second leg. The crowd was 136,505, which remains the record for any UEFA match.

How difficult was it to sneak in to Hampden?

As these photos show, not very difficult at all. A stadium this size is going to have weak spots.

Above is the Auld Enemy game of 1978. On the right, a gate is breached allowing supporters to pour in to the 1970 Celtic v Aberdeen Scottish Cup Final. Thousands got in (although some may actually have had tickets and just took a short-cut) before these gates were forced shut again.

And youngsters were always lifted over turnstiles.

Which throws up an intriguing question: if it was this easy, how many did it over the years? How many more spectators than are listed in official attendances for big games were actually in the ground?

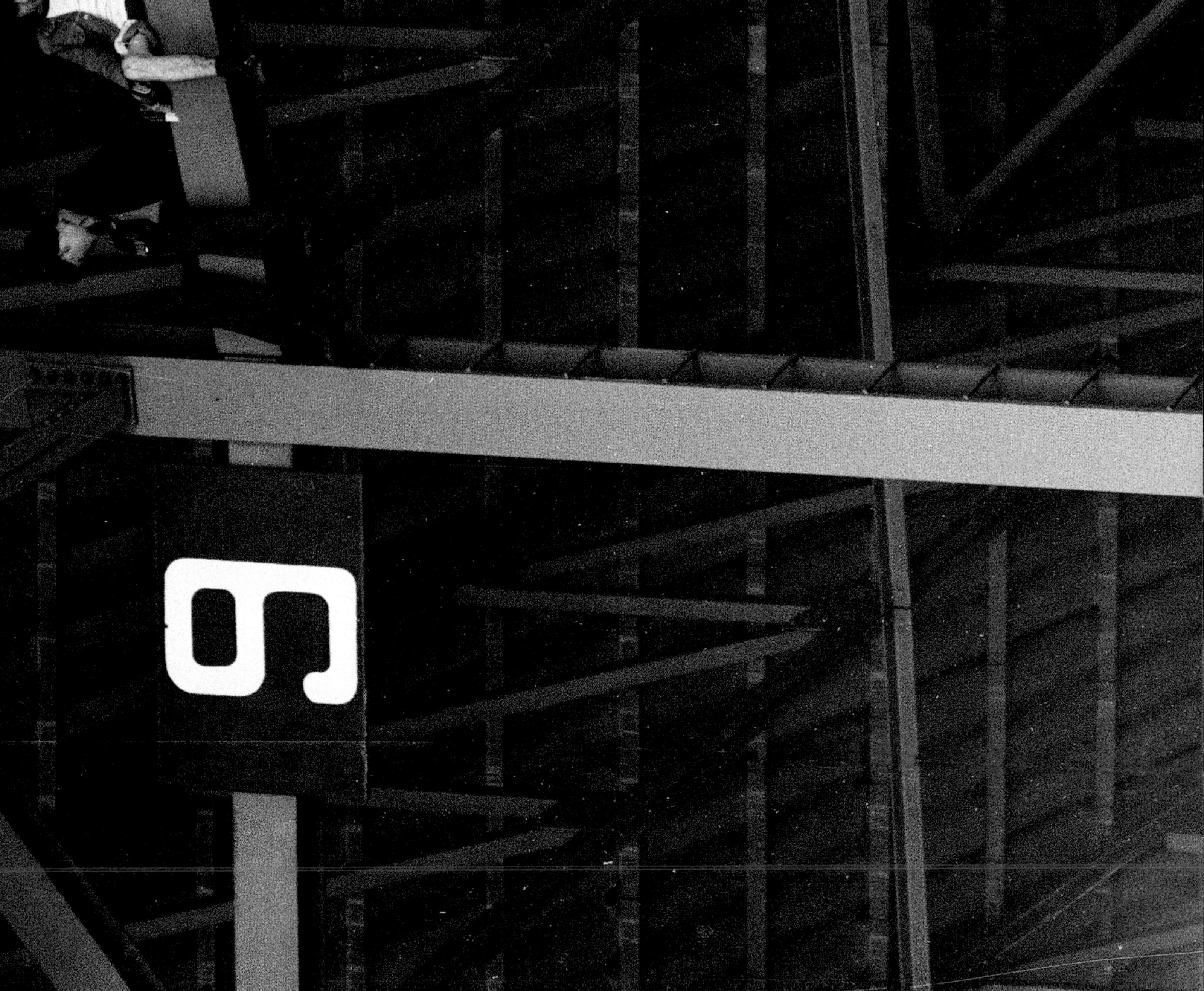

■ Apologies, you'll have had to turn your book on its side to see this photo properly. Once inside Hampden, among those huge crowds, you had to somehow find a spot that had a good view. These lads, perched high in the roof girders of the Mount Florida end, were taking it to dangerous extremes. This is the "wish you well for Argentina" Scotland v England game of May 20th, 1978.

■ There were ways to see the game if you didn't have a ticket. This page shows Hampden from the Somerville Drive tenements. And, right, from the Battlefield Court flats.

■ **Racing Club of Argentina training at Hampden before the notorious World Club match of 1967 against Celtic. The Mount Florida end roof is under construction, a painful view-blocker for those on the previous page living in the overlooking tenements.**

Note Hampden's crush barriers, which are very similar to the Ibrox barriers. They were of the patented Archie Leitch design (see page 58).

Three of Hampden's subterranean entry/exit tunnels are also apparent towards the rear of the terracing.

A position at the wall behind one of these was a plum spot which guaranteed a good view and a wall to lean on during a game. You had to be in early to get a place, though.

There were six of these entries, at walkways 10, 12, 15, 17, 19 and 21, though none at the east end of the ground. They were only used by Leitch when lack of space didn't allow stairs behind the terrace.

The sturdy iron fence between the north terracing and the Mount Florida end was a long-standing feature of Hampden even before crowd segregation measures (see page 334) became widely used in Scottish football grounds.

■ On October 31st, 1953, Queen's Park marked the 50th anniversary of the opening of this (the third) Hampden by inviting former players and VIPs to the day's game. They included Bill Struth (Rangers), Willie Maley (Celtic), Paddy Travers (Clyde and Aberdeen), Jimmy McMenemy (Celtic and Partick), Alex Currie (Queen's Park and Airdrie), Andrew Richmond (Queen's Park and Rangers), Willie Loney (Celtic) and James McAlpine (Queen's Park's record goalscorer and later club president). That collection of names heard long ago was probably the most stellar gathering there ever was of the greats of Scottish football of the first half of the 20th Century. Unfortunately, Queen's lost their B Division game 4-2 to Ayr (right) before a sparse 4,000 crowd.

138

■ **The early-1980s work.**

It took many years, but eventually Hampden grew to be a wreck. Eight decades of hard use had taken a toll.

There had been Government promises of help to rebuild, but the money never came. Frankly, we were badly let-down after what had seemed to be concrete arrangements.

By the 1980s, properly organised segregation, sanitary arrangements, modern seating, disabled access and better facilities in almost all areas of the ground were required. The old place was no longer fit for purpose.

What had once been the pride of the nation had become a problem and an eyesore. Extensive refurbishment work was undertaken.

The grand old lady, as she had been, passed away.

■ The fall of the north stand and enclosure. This photo was taken on July 23rd, 1982.

■ The 1990s rebuild.

Ten years later, the march of time demanded further work. There was debate over whether the huge sums required to modernise made it viable for Hampden to continue to be Scotland's national stadium. But eventually, after much wrangling, work started.

These photos were taken on April 21st, 1993, and show the last glimpses of the great old stadium as a place where so many stood to watch football.

The old Hampden, with all its glories and all its faults.

It wasn't perfect.

Indeed, in places and at times it was downright dangerous – some of the people perched on the back wall in this photo are one crowd sway away from a nasty fall.

And there was many a broken ankle and bruised rib after wild goal celebrations.

The view wasn't great in some areas. The queues to get in could be horrendous. The queues to buy tickets were even worse.

It was filthy. You came out looking like you'd been standing in a ploughed field for a couple of hours. And the toilet facilities would have had to rise several notches to be described as rudimentary.

And yet there were some great times on those shallow terraces. The famous Hampden Roar was a thing of awesome power in its day.

To attend a big game was a memorable experience. One that football fans of today can never have.

You never forget your first visit to Hampden Park.

As can be seen, the wings of the old main stand were at slightly different angles. This was a Leitch design habit, the same feature can be seen in the North Stand.

The south "kink" was left over from the days when there had been two South Stands, with a pavilion in the middle.

The stand enclosure (right) and huge north enclosure, following the same lines, were a little deeper in the middle than at the ends, though it was only really discernible on the south side.

On the far left, the arched undercroft of the terrace can be seen, which led to the two mid-terrace entrances at the Mount Florida end.

The east end, furthest away in these photos, was able to have extension terracing at the top because there was more room behind it.

There were no mid-terrace entries at that end for the same reason, but outside stairways and sloped paths that ran off sideways to the north and south.

Lesser Hampden

QUEEN'S PARK bought a patch of land from Clincart Farm on the west side of Hampden Park in 1923 to use as a pitch for their Strollers (the reserve team). It became Lesser Hampden and at its peak had a 12,000 capacity.

The farmhouse (in the background of next page) was converted into dressing rooms and though now not used is believed to be the oldest building in any football stadium in the world.

Scotland sometimes trained at Lesser Hampden, and would also give visiting national sides the run of the place.

During the Second World War, Lesser Hampden was commandeered for use as a base for a Home Guard detachment. The Dad's Army platoon hatched a plan to plough up the pitch and plant potatoes to ease any forthcoming food shortages. Thankfully, this did not prove to be necessary.

■ **Left: April 1952, a gaggle of USA defenders make a better job of challenging for high balls in training than they did in the game next day, when they lost 6-0 to Scotland in front of 107,765 at the big Hampden..**

■ **Right: Portugal's star striker Matateu (dubbed "the world's eighth wonder") limbers up at Lesser Hampden before a friendly with Scotland in May 1955.**

This was a famous occasion in the black and white era. It was 1961, the Italian League came to play the Scottish League, bringing our own Denis Law (Torino, a £110,000 buy from Manchester City) with them.

In the Italian team were Britons (left-to-right below) Gerry Hitchens (Inter Milan, an £85,000 buy from Aston Villa), John Charles (Juventus, a £65,000 buy from Leeds United), Denis, and Joe Baker (Torino, a £75,000 buy from Hibs).

They are pictured at Lesser Hampden on October 31st. The game the next evening in front of a soaked 67,996 at the big Hampden was a 1-1 draw, Ralph Brand for Scotland, Hitchens for Italy.

Falkirk

A GREAT Scottish ground, Brockville Park. It is gone but will never be forgotten. It was Falkirk Football Club's home from 1885 until 2003.

But the old place was left behind by the march of time and ever-changing stadium standards.

Failure to meet the new requirements was the reason the club, despite being successful on the pitch, were controversially denied promotion to the Scottish Premier League.

In 2002-03 The Bairns had won Division One at a canter but the new Falkirk Stadium wasn't ready.

Despite interventions by MPs, a 12,000-name petition, and angry protestations from any football person who had a sense of fair play, the authorities (the newly-formed SPL, known to many as the Self-Preservation League) wouldn't budge. Rules are rules when po-faced officialdom has power to wield.

The Bairns were kept down in Division One.

In any case, Brockville was well on its way to becoming a supermarket by then.

Falkirk have moved on – the last game at Brockville was a 3-2 loss to ICT on May 10th, 2004.

A lone, blue-painted turnstile now stands in the Morrisons store car park to mark what was the home of the twice Scottish Cup winners.

■ Falkirk v Celtic on September 21st, 1963. Falkirk won 1-0, with captain Willie Fulton scoring a cracking 25-yarder.

■ **Falkirk v Rangers on January 18th, 1969. A 3-0 win for the visitors in a Division 1 game that featured a mass brawl which, once the punches stopped, resulted in Falkirk's John Markie and Rangers' Willie Johnston being sent off. There was officially a 22,000 crowd, though Brockville wasn't too difficult to climb in to in those days. The small shed at the right-hand corner in this photo was the schoolboys' corner. Brockville, as a stadium, had an X-factor – that difficult-to-define thing they call "character". The crowd**

was very close to the pitch, held back by just a two-bar fence, and the choir that stood under the long Hope Street terrace roof on the left of this photo would generate an incredible amount of noise. Quips from the regulars could be heard by the players, and would sometimes even be answered back. Supporters stood at their favourite spot year after year, decade after decade. When Scottish football fans talk of the charms and charisma to be found in the old terraced grounds, it is the likes of Brockville that they mean.

■ The glorious Falkirk 1957 Scottish Cup-winning team in front of the long terrace opposite Brockville's main stand. From left: Derek Grierson, Eddie O'Hara, Tommy Murray, Dougie Moran, Jim McIntosh (reserve on the day), Andy Irvine, Bert Slater, Ian Rae, John Prentice and George Merchant. Missing are Alex Parker, who was on National Service, and Alex Wright, who was absent the day this pic was taken.

■ Half-back Len Fletcher trains in 1955 while maintenance is done on the stand behind him.

■ Troubled times. That's a thrown pint glass that the ref has in his hand. With the thoughtlessly brave, displeased schoolmaster-type approach of referees of the old days he is about to lecture the supporters on their unacceptable behavior. A good shot of Brockville's original floodlights in the background.

Brockville's biggest crowd, 23,100, saw one of the legendary events of Scottish football. It was a Cup Third Round tie on February 21st, 1953. The Bairns were two up at half-time, inspired by 38-year-old Jimmy Delaney, former darling of the Celtic support.

Celtic were awarded a corner seven minutes into the second half and Irishman Charlie Tully scored direct from it. However, the referee disallowed this, ruling the ball hadn't been properly placed.

The crowd had spilled out over the railings after the "goal" and Tully had to usher several out the way – and also reposition a not-very-pleased-about-it policeman – to re-take the corner. He sent an identical inswinger straight into the net again!

Celtic scored another through Willie Fernie, then John McGrory got the winner which sparked such a crowd invasion and "piley-on" that McGrory needed treatment before he could play on.

■ **Jimmy Delaney playing for Falkirk, though not in that famous 1953 game (unfortunately, this is a badly cracked glass negative).**

Hibernian

THE huge East Terrace at Easter Road, when full, was one of the most awe-inspiring sights of Scottish football.

The "back" of the terrace was added in the early 1950s, during a great period for Hibs, the Famous Five era, and the ground's biggest ever crowd rolled up to see them play an Edinburgh New Year derby on January 2nd, 1950.

The circumstances around the game are stark illustrations of how crowd management has changed in the seven decades since.

In those days the police had the biggest part in saying when the ground was full. This time, they let too many in.

The crowd was officially given as 65,850 though many who were there say they reckon possibly 10,000 more had got inside the stadium. The back of the East Terrace wasn't even at its full height by that point, making the crushing even worse.

Schoolboys were milling all round the track, unable to find a place on the terraces. Amazingly, the police attempted to solve this with mounted charges to clear the pitch. This resulted in more than 50 fans, many of them children, being stretchered out by First Aid men. One man collapsed and later died. Hearts won the game 2-1.

Hibs were duelling with Rangers for the title but would lose the 1949-50 League championship by a single point.

■ **This photo of a packed East Terrace is Hibs v Celtic on October 8th, 1966, when the crowd was only 43,256.**

■ Another photo of the East Terracing, taken from the other end. In its time this was the biggest single expanse of terracing in British football (if the top and bottom sections are regarded as one). Pic shows a visit from Celtic on October 9th, 1971, with a 41,000 crowd.

■ Hibs keeper Tommy Younger rushes out to perform what was seen as the measure of valour for a keeper, a dive at the feet of an on-rushing striker. Everyone held their breath as memories of the John Thomson incident were still fresh.

The Aberdeen forward is winger Allan Boyd, who played for Great Britain at the 1948 Olympics.

The defender is Jock Paterson, stalwart centre-half of the great Hibs teams of the 1950s. He was the father of Craig Paterson, a renowned defender in his own right who played for Hibs, Rangers and Motherwell in the '80s and '90s.

■ Scotland B v England B at Easter Road on Wednesday, March 11, 1953. The attendance, for a midweek 3pm kick-off, was 16,975. It was a 2-2 draw. In this photo, showing the Dunbar End in the background, Dundee's Doug Cowie chases Bill Holden, of Burnley.

■ The south end of Easter Road, with the big scoreboard, during a 2-1 Edinburgh derby win for Hibs on September 7th, 1974. Hibs also missed two penalties that day but went joint top of the First Division, albeit after only two games of the season.

■ The old main stand, on the west side of Easter Road. This photo was taken in 1994, just before work started to reconstruct both ends of the stadium.

Easter Road opened in 1893, but Hibernian very nearly moved out in 1909 when plans for a huge stadium at Piershill, about a mile further south, were unveiled.

The problem was that Hibs didn't own the land where Easter Road was situated, so the attraction of a new ground was strong.

The Piershill blueprint was for a 50,000-capacity stadium, with room to expand even further.

However, the North British Railway Company won a court order allowing them to build a new rail line over the proposed site.

Hibs had no choice (the railway companies were hugely politically powerful at that time) but to give way. Frustratingly, the railway line was never actually built.

However, now determined to stay put, the club negotiated a better and longer deal with their landlord. A remodelled ground, completed by the new main stand with its distinctive slight curve and bench seats, was built between 1922 and 1924.

The work suffered several delays due to strike action and materials shortages following the First World War but the result became one of Scottish football's iconic and most historically significant grounds.

■ The North end of Easter Road during an Edinburgh derby, on September 9th, 1972.

In an attempt to combat "rowdyism", and prevent the usual suspects congregating in their favoured place, the club had closed off the cow shed with a fence.

■ The temporary closure didn't work. This is a couple of lads (not home supporters) being lifted during Hibs' 3-1 defeat of Rangers in a League Cup sectional tie on August 10th, 1974. Hibs got to the final that year. The boys' bad behaviour allows us a good look into the nether regions of the long-gone cow shed.

■ **Hibs brought George Best to Easter Road in 1979. It was a move that amazed all of Scotland. This is the great man in a league game with Celtic on January 12th, 1980, a 1-1 draw in which Best scored (opposite page) and won a penalty (though it was missed by Ally McLeod). The crowd was 21,936.**

Whisky

BUY DUNCAN'S HA

CHOCOLATE

■ Of course George Best is far from the only star to have graced Easter Road. Fans of an older vintage will tell you much better players have played in Leith. Above: Lawrie Reilly in front of the main stand in 1954.

And, arguably, perhaps the most naturally gifted Hibee of them all. Gordon Smith is seen here showing his team-mates the new lightweight kit Hibs would wear while on their forthcoming foreign summer tour.

Gretna

A ROCKET that climbed high, burned bright, then just as quickly fizzled out. There are many stories, true and false, surrounding the rise and fall of Gretna. Just to add to the (sometimes bizarre) legends surrounding the club, their record crowd is a lie.

After half a century in English football the club were elected to the Scottish League system in 2002 then fell under the influence of Brooks Mileson, an insurance industry tycoon. They were storming up the leagues when they drew top-flight Dundee United in the Scottish Cup Third Round, in January 2005. A temporary stand was built for the game, taking the normal 2,200 capacity of Raydale Park to 3,000.

Mileson purchased all the home tickets, effectively making the game free entry, though it was never clear who was holding these tickets locally as the total population of Gretna is only around 2,700.

United supporters were set to travel in numbers but the first game was postponed because of snow storms. By the time the tie was played, nine days later on Monday, January 17th, the weather was still very bad. The attendance is recorded as 3,000 because that's how many tickets were "sold", but there was nothing like that in the ground. United won 4-3 in what was a very good game, even if played in freezing conditions.

Raydale's second biggest (and probably actual biggest) was 2,307 in an FA Cup tie. Gretna played Rochdale in the first round in November 1991, having battled through four qualifying rounds. They earned a creditable 0-0 home draw with The Dale, then in the English Fourth Division, before going down 3-1 in the replay.

Gretna reached the Scottish Cup Final in 2006 (losing to Hearts on penalties) and spent the 2007-08 season in the top league.

But Mileson withdrew support due to health reasons and a debt reported to be as high as £9 million put the club out of business in June 2008. A phoenix club, Gretna 2008, now play in the Lowland League.

JOHN DAVIDSON BAKERS LTD

Third Lanark

CATHKIN PARK is the name that doomsayers and administrators use when they are trying to scare over-spending club chairmen. It is like referencing the bogeyman in a fairy tale: "You wouldn't want to end up like Third Lanark, would you?"

And it is, indeed, a frightening prospect. The story of the team that died still sends cold shivers through the supporters of all other Scottish clubs.

The remains of Cathkin Park can still be seen, just over the hill from Hampden, though it is well over half a century since the Hi-Hi kicked their last ball.

Thirds had known great days. Their record attendance was 45,591 for a Scottish Cup Third Round tie against Rangers on February 27th, 1954 – and Thirds were a Second Division club at the time.

That was a stinker of a game, one of those that are described as having "defences on top". The final score was 0-0, with chances few and far between.

The replay, the following Wednesday was, by contrast, a cracker. It finished 4-4 after extra time. The second replay (again at Ibrox on the Monday five days later) was almost as good, Rangers winning 3-2.

■ **Left: Jocky Henderson of Thirds, followed by Jim MacEwan of Raith Rovers, trudge towards the Cathkin Park pavilion. The two were sent off after an "incident in the goalmouth while a corner was coming in" on February 14th, 1953. Thirds won this A Division relegation dogfight 2-1, but it was the Glasgow club who were relegated at the end of that season.**

■ April 10th, 1965. The new main stand at Cathkin Park, with a crowd of less than 1,000. They were watching Thirds take on Dunfermline. Pars striker, Alex Ferguson, who would become the greatest manager football has ever known, put this shot just past Evan Williams' post. Thirds would again be relegated at the end of this season, and this time would never return. Note the TV gantry under the new roof.

■ **One of the greats of Thirds history, right-back Matt Balunas, shepherds the ball away from Aberdeen's Don Emery in 1950 with Cathkin Park's not-yet-roofed south terracing in the background.**

■ He is remembered as a charismatic manager, but outside-left Ally MacLeod was a Thirds pin-up before his transfer to St Mirren in 1955. Before his move our photographer was despatched to capture his mesmerising footwork and left-footed accuracy with a dead ball – and got great shots of Cathkin Park in the background.

■ **1960. Competitive hoopla in front of Cathkin Park's old stand. Thirds had just recruited several full-time players at this point. The ambition to be a big club was clear.**

■ August 1964. Inside-left David Kerr doing laps. The former Liverpool man had a brief stay at Thirds. This terracing is (mostly) still there, though overgrown. Anyone interested in football history should have a look at Cathkin Park. Be warned, however, the grave of a once-proud club is a sad place.

The entirety of Scottish football was diminished by the loss of Third Lanark. The Hi-Hi were a major club, with tens of thousands of supporters. Some of these will have gone to follow other teams, but some were lost to the game.

The blame is laid at the feet of Bill Hiddleston, club chairman when Thirds were liquidated. Many entirely justified harsh words have been directed his way. There had been financial irregularities for years but the crux was the £50,000 spent replacing Cathkin Park's 19th Century grandstand (pictured here) at a time when attendances were falling, along with Thirds' playing fortunes. At the time the stand was being planned Thirds had one of the best teams in Scotland – hence the provision of a TV gantry.

Tragically, this would hardly be used as Thirds spent their last two seasons in the Second Division.

But there should have been, and still should be, tighter regulation on the running of football clubs.

The loss of a club is not just the loss of a business. No other social entity gives a community such a

common cause to rally round – think what it does to any town when its club reaches the cup final.

You have a right to your football club.

Whenever football is talked about in our wee country, supporters must be taken into account. The mental health, wellbeing, and sense of belonging of thousands of us has to be considered.

The demise of Thirds shouldn't have happened, and shouldn't have been allowed to happen. And it should never be allowed to happen again.

■ **Matt Balunas and Raith Rovers' Ernie Copland tussle before a 14,000-crowd at Cathkin Park on March 15th, 1952.**

■ Elbows ref! George Young, the former Rangers legend, was manager of Thirds from 1959 to 1962. He is seen here giving Matt Gray and Dave Hilley tips on challenging for a high ball.

The south terracing, behind, was able to accommodate huge numbers under cover.

■ Cathkin Park had (along with Airdrie's Broomfield) one of the last pavilions in Scottish football. But by April 1968, a few months after the Hi-Hi were liquidated, the pavilion and most of the ground had fallen into an irretrievable state. It's enough to make a grown man weep.

Albion Rovers

THE biggest crowd to ever fit in to Cliftonhill was 27,381 for a Scottish Cup Second Round tie against Rangers on February 8th, 1936. Falkirk (v Kilmarnock) and Elgin (v Queen of the South) also set new attendance records that Saturday.

Rangers, on their way to winning the Cup for a third year running, won 3-1

Rovers were mid-table in the First Division and had a storming first half. They led 1-0 at the break through a Jimmy Rice header. It might have been even better but for Willie Bruce missing a penalty at 0-0.

But what is true today was true then. If you don't take your chances, big teams punish you. Rangers got a stern talking-to from Bill Struth and came out a different side after the break. Jimmy Simpson equalised and a double from the hyper-prolific Jimmy Smith saw the Ibrox side home.

■ **Left and above: The enclosure opposite Cliftonhill's main stand in 1961. The roof had stood at the Coatbridge end since 1954, before being moved to the side of the pitch in 1959. It blew down in the deadly Hurricane Low Q of January 1968 but was rebuilt the following close-season.**

Outside grounds

THESE are bits of football history that journalists, players, managers, and club officials rarely think about and only ever saw in passing. But for fans the turnstiles, the queues, the approaches to the ground, the view from outside, was an integral part of football.

When you remember the old grounds you picture the games and players, of course. But you also remember the experience of arriving at the ground, the impatient (and slightly worried about getting in at all if it wasn't an all-ticket match) wait for admittance, the smells of the burger vans (in later years), and the shouts of the hawkers – err ra macaroon bars!

The metal clicking of the turnstiles and the few steps forward every minute were extra ratchets to enhance the experience.

You will also recall the sound of the crowd already inside, which is a cherished experience that has been lost to football. It has been drowned out by the fixation on playing loud music. They even try to drown out goal celebrations.

In the old days, as you arrived the sound of the chants from inside the ground mushroomed your excitement. People would join in with the singing while still standing in line. It stoked the battle fever, it made the game real. It got us going.

And it was even better at a night game. The gloom added a sense of danger, pierced only slightly by floodlights that weren't really intended to light the outer areas of the ground. Who was alongside you? What colours were they wearing?

It was all part of going to the game. It was living.

Why on earth did clubs kill all of this with incessant music loud enough to drown out conversation even outside grounds?

Did they take account of how fans enjoyed games, and what – exactly – it was that made the game so exciting for us?

Did they ever truly look at football from a fan's perspective? Did they ever queue to pay their few bob, hear the banter, feel the impatience, get high on the mounting anticipation?

Sadly, few photos of the outside of grounds survive. Photographers were concerned with action on the pitch, and important people like players and managers. Camera film was expensive, not to be wasted on the hoi polloi. It was rare to point a lens at the poor punters trying to get in, or the streets around the grounds.

So this is what I have. The few pictures in this chapter are all that remain to evoke memories that will die with us and then be lost forever.

This was football, this was.

■ Queues down Edward Street (with police horses ploughing them into line) for the Scottish Cup Third Round tie between Motherwell and Rangers on Saturday, February 25th, 1961. A crowd of 31,958 saw a thrilling 2-2 draw. 'Well would win the replay 5-2 at Ibrox the following Wednesday in front of 90,000.

■ Hampden, May 25th, 1985. Scotland v. England. We, the cattle, negotiate six-inch-deep puddles as we wait for the privilege of getting into a game that we, the fans, made into one of the greatest, and most lucrative, spectacles on the world football calendar. Mind you, Scotland won 1-0 so no one minded!

■ **Rangers supporters walking up Carseview Road to get to Forfar's Station Park for a Scottish Cup Second Round tie on February 7th, 1970. They are being filtered through a check-point and searched for weapons. Police also assessed their state of sobriety. Rangers won the game 7-0. See also page 208.**

■ Muirton, the back of the stand on Dunkeld Road in the early 1980s. The back was a brick-and-mortar wall but the steps and seats of the stand inside were wooden and a large part of it was closed after the Bradford City fire in 1985. Of the 2,185 seats, only 500 were left for use. In those dark days, Muirton saw its lowest ever crowd, 466 for a Second Division game against Albion Rovers on April 19th, 1986.

■ **1958.** The painted-on goal, with its target areas, at the Watson Street End of Falkirk's Brockville, created by the deep-thinking (and years ahead of his time) "Professor" Reggie Smith – whose methods could not be questioned as he had managed The Bairns to their 1957 Scottish Cup win. The red ash park was often used by the club for training, though it wasn't the best of surfaces, and became a car park on match days.

200

COWDENBEATH F.C. LTD. CENTRAL PARK.

O MONEY RETURNED UNDER ANY CIRCUMSTANCES

ADMISSION

PLEASE HAVE CORRECT MONEY READY

ADMISSION

■ **Left: a photo taken outside Central Park, Cowdenbeath, in 1968 to mark Andy Matthew's elevation to become 'Beath manager.**

The legend above the turnstiles reads: "No money returned under any circumstances" – you wouldn't get your three shillings back easily from a Fifer!

Cowdenbeath were far from alone in treating fans like this.

It was always a struggle to get money back or vouchers if games had kicked off, but were abandoned due to heavy snowfalls or fog (it was unheard of for games to be abandoned for mere gales, or any amount of rainfall short of a deluge that would frighten Noah).

And you'd look long and hard to find a club with a customer relations department.

■ **Right: Partick Thistle's Firhill, with police horses on hand to control the huge and dangerous crowds.**

■ **Supporters' buses going to Dens and Tannadice would park at Gussie Park. This is a Rangers visit to Dundee United in 1979. Bus trips were when songs would be composed, and carry-outs consumed. If you went to the fitba in the 1960s or '70s you'll know what these wild away days were like, and you'll know that some of the old stories should never be re-told!**

■ One of the all-time-great Scottish football photos. The quite remarkable queue on Merkland Road, taken from atop the gates of Pittodrie, for the 1935 Scottish Cup Quarter-Final between Aberdeen and Celtic.

■ Pittodrie again, March 18th, 1953. The queues to get into an Aberdeen-Hibs Scottish Cup Quarter-Final replay that had already kicked-off when this photo was taken, with fans perched on advertising hoardings. The crowd was more than 42,000. The Dons won 2-0 and would go on to beat Third Lanark in the semi, but lose the final to Rangers after a replay.

■ The turnstiles and main gate at the rear of Airdrieonians' famous old pavilion, pictured just before the club moved away from Broomfield in 1994. Behind this wall lay the curved terrace behind the goal, with its unusually wide terrace steps, the two-barred crush barriers that many fans would sit on, and the strange far end that was lower in the middle but higher at each corner. It's all gone.

■ Not all of what went on outside was good. There were dangers in the streets surrounding the ground which would have few, if any, police. You had to keep your wits about you. This photo shows fans outside an off-licence near Ibrox before the Old Firm game of September 15th, 1973. Fighting fuel is being poured down throats. There was trouble at the game. Beer cans were thrown and fans spilled on to the pitch.

Forfar Athletic

THE Loons moved in to Station Park in 1888, three years after they formed, and have been there ever since – despite the occasional wind storm blowing the stand away (see Weather chapter in Volume 3).

The biggest crowd the ground ever held was on February 7th, 1970, when 10,782 saw a cup tie against Rangers.

The visitors had recently appointed Willie Waddell as manager. It was his tenth game, the previous nine being eight wins and one draw (at Celtic Park).

A hungry Rangers faithful were fired with enthusiasm, hoping their new man could break the Jock Stein-inspired procession of green and white titles. They travelled in huge numbers to Angus and confidence was boosted again by the result of the game, a 7-0 thrashing that included a John Greig double.

■ **The photo on the right shows Station Park's newly-built stand just before the teams ran out for another cup tie against Rangers, on January 31st, 1959. Note the wooden barrier. Rangers won 3-1 that cold day, in front of a crowd of 9,813.**

The sheet held up on the left-hand side of the photo is for charitable donations. Spectators would throw in pennies as it went round the track.

Arbroath

THE biggest crowd ever to descend upon Gayfield was the 13,510, who saw a Scottish Cup Third Round tie against Rangers on February 23rd, 1952.

Arbroath were bottom of the B Division at the time (and remained thereabouts all season) while Rangers were third in the A Division, though with games in hand. The Glasgow club would be runners-up to champions Hibs that year.

But the Red Lichties gave a very good account of themselves, inspired by what was described as "a quiet talk" given to the players before the game setting out the club's proud cup traditions.

They went a goal down early, Willie Thornton getting on the scoresheet as he almost always did. But Arbroath took control after that.

Rangers' Iron Curtain defence took a dent when George Young injured his shoulder and played the rest of the game with his arm strapped across his chest.

But Arbroath couldn't find a goal and another header from Thornton made the final score 2-0.

■ **Gayfield 1960. Once you were through the turnstiles at Arbroath's venerable and historical old ground, you saw the back of the stand. It is much changed nowadays, with cabins in front and floodlight pylons on the roof. The only adornment six decades ago was the manager's bike. This photo was taken before the floodlights were put up – but after the disastrous events described on the next four pages.**

■ In the early hours of Thursday, September 18th, 1958, a fire broke out in the Gayfield stand. Arbroath had played Partick Thistle in a League Cup Quarter-Final second leg a few hours previously. The club was determined the next scheduled Division Two game, against Berwick Rangers two days later, would go ahead. So a massive clean-up operation was undertaken, the debris taken away and the ground made safe.

■ The players got changed at Arbroath Lads Club pavilion on Alexandra Place, and walked to the game. They are shown above making their way down the grassy hill past the famous Tuttie's Neuk pub across the road from Gayfield. The Arbroath players are, from left, John Brown, Bill Nicoll, Jim Fraser lagging behind, Willie McLean, goalkeeper Bobby Williamson and Ronnie Sharp.

■ The Red Lichties beat the Wee Rangers 2-0 that day, and would storm to promotion that season. However, the cost to world football of this one, fairly small, fire was devastating. All of Arbroath's memorabilia was lost, including photos and other mementoes from the record 36-0 victory over Bon Accord of 1885.

East Fife

THE Fifers' record crowd at their old Bayview Park was a great day for the club. Not only did they pull in 22,515 spectators but they thrashed their local rivals Raith Rovers.

January 2nd, 1950, was the first top-flight New Year clash between the two since 1931. The home side, enjoying the best period in their history under Scot Symon and with five full Scottish internationals in the team, ran out 3-0 winners.

The huge crowd saw a brilliant performance from Methil magician Allan Brown at inside-forward. He was soon to join Blackpool for £26,500, the largest fee that had ever been received by a Scottish club at that time.

The crowd on that 1950 day was partly made possible by concrete anti-tank blocks East Fife had transported from Leven beach. They were used to heighten the terracing at the west end of the ground.

■ **This photo shows Kenny Dalglish attempting a shot in front of an 11,577 crowd at Bayview for the visit of Celtic on February 17th, 1973. This was a renowned game in Scottish football folklore, a 2-2 league draw in which Celtic missed three penalties with three different takers (Bobby Murdoch, Harry Hood and Dalglish) inside a 12-minute period.**

■ An easier visit for Celtic than the one shown on the previous page. An 18-year-old Gordon Durie can't prevent Mark Reid getting in a cross during a 6-0 Scottish Cup Fourth Round win on February 18th, 1984. This was a game lit up by a commanding Tommy Burns performance.

East Fife moved in to Bayview in 1903. There was the stand but only turf banking round the other three sides until 1923, when terracing was installed.

Eventually, with the old place becoming a bit run down but the central location in Methil and development of the surrounding area making the site attractive to a supermarket chain, the club agreed to sell at the end of the 1997-98 season. They moved across town to the 1,980-capacity New Bayview.

■ **Above: 1958, manager Charlie McCaig conducts heading practice on the Bayview pitch.**

Dumbarton

THE biggest crowd ever to attend Boghead saw the visit of Raith Rovers for a Scottish Cup Quarter-Final on March 2nd, 1957. This puts The Sons among the few west-of-Scotland clubs whose record crowd doesn't involve a visit from the Old Firm.

The Sons had been going well in the cup that 1957 season, beating Queen of the South and then shocking the powerful "Ancell Babes" Motherwell 3-1 at Fir Park on the way to the game against Rovers.

The 18,001 people turning up at Boghead that day was a surprise to everyone – even though the crowd for the glorious win over Motherwell had been above 16,000 with a very impressive Sons travelling support.

Vast queues formed outside the ground for the Rovers game, with a huge Fife contingent coming in.

The Kirkcaldy side were enjoying one of their best ever seasons, having beaten Dundee United 7-0 to get to the quarter-final. They would finish fourth in the 1956-57 First Division, their best since placing third in 1921-22. Dumbarton were mid-table in the Second Division.

Rovers won the game 4-0, and played the last 15 minutes with 10 men as keeper Charlie Drummond went off with a cut eye that needed five stitches after he dived at the feet of The Sons' Hughie Gallacher.

Boghead had one of Scottish football's more romantic terracing covers behind the goal. It was the former platform roof from Turnberry Railway Station with Victorian metalwork of a far more ornate design than was usually seen in the girders-and-corrugated-iron style of architecture the Scottish fitba fan is used to.

The structure was erected at the station in 1906, though it closed in 1942. The roof wasn't sold to the club until 1957 so had remained in place at the unused station for 15 years.

But, in an era before vandalism had been invented, it was as good as new.

■ **Right: The queues outside Boghead for that 1957 record attendance.**

■ There isn't a date for this late-1950s game at Boghead, although with The Sons of the Rock in hooped yellow-and-black shirts it must be before the 1960-61 season, as they adopted a vertical stripe that year.

The photo was kindly donated by the family of Sons fan Robert Strachan (1926-2000), a former York City director, FA official and UEFA inspector.

■ Dumbarton v Aberdeen at Boghead, October 13th, 1973.

Aberdeen won 1-0, with a goal from Drew Jarvie (seen here up for a header). The crowd was estimated at 4,000.

The 80-seat Postage Box stand would be replaced in 1980 with a larger, 303-capacity stand.

But Dumbarton would move from Boghead at the end of the 1999-2000 season, playing at Albion Rovers' Cliftonhill until December when the new Dumbarton Football Stadium (known to fans as The Rock) was ready for use.

The last game at the old ground was against East Fife on May 6th, 2000, in front of a 3,000 crowd. The Rock has a single, all-seated stand which holds 2,000.

■ **Dumbarton v Celtic, November 24th, 1973.** A 2-0 win for the visitors, notable for Bobby Lennox scoring his 241st goal to break Stevie Chalmers' post-war record for Celtic. Bobby would finish his career with a total of 301 goals. The bonny ironwork of the old train station roof can be seen at Boghead's far end.

Real football

FOOTBALL exists outwith the Scottish Professional Football Leagues.

The senior game consists of the four divisions we have nowadays, though there were only two until 1975, and three until 1994. Then there are organisations like the Highland League (formed in 1893), the East of Scotland League (1923), and the South of Scotland League (1946). The Scottish Junior Football Association was formed in 1886.

In this football pyramid, the drawing power of the wider game is worthy of respect. The Scottish Junior Cup final of 1950-51 attracted 77,560 to Hampden to see Petershill beat Irvine Meadow 1-0. But that was just one of the 50,000-plus crowds the Junior Cup Final attracted in the 1950s and '60s.

The history of the various leagues, especially the Junior leagues, their formations, dissolutions and amalgamations, would require a book of its own.

There was also a plethora of district cups, many of which used to be contested by senior clubs.

Raith Rovers, for instance, will recall the six times they lifted the Penman Cup (the last being 1958-59), while St Johnstone would point to their half-dozen victories in the Reid Cup, though they last won it in 1895-96.

But there are many clubs who never played in the senior set-up but who fought their way through the decades with ingenuity, dedication and sacrifices made by armies of volunteers and enthusiasts.

The players played for what is often romantically termed a love of the game, though money was (and still is) paid in the Juniors. But no Corinthian, wholesome description can fully explain Junior football. It is a way to satisfy a fierce need to play and to win.

Football is an obsession, and nowhere is that more starkly shown than in the levels of commitment in a tough game played by two teams of hard, hard men.

This was the reason why crowds came to lower league games. The football was real. Every ground in this chapter has hosted a game, a thousand games, which turned into raw, aggressive, blood-and-snotters battles. But, and this must be stressed, there was always good football and highly skilled players in the Junior ranks too, and in the other leagues shown here.

And they played in characterful, interesting (though sometimes scruffy) stadiums.

However, it is a sad fact that several of the clubs shown here are no longer with us. Sustaining life at this level was always a precarious business.

These clubs had long histories at grounds they owned and maintained, sometimes for a century or more. These places were bastions of Scottish football and deserve to be celebrated. This chapter is a tribute to the wider game in Scotland in the black and white era.

My thanks and respects go to a real football man, Jim Kidd, for the majority of the photos.

■ **Right: 1965. The Scottish Junior Cup Final at Hampden. A 10,000 crowd saw Linlithgow Rose beat Baillieston 4-1.**

■ Strathspey Thistle's Seafield Park.

■ Carnoustie Panmure's Westfield Park.

■ Baillieston's Station Park.

■ Spartans' City Park.

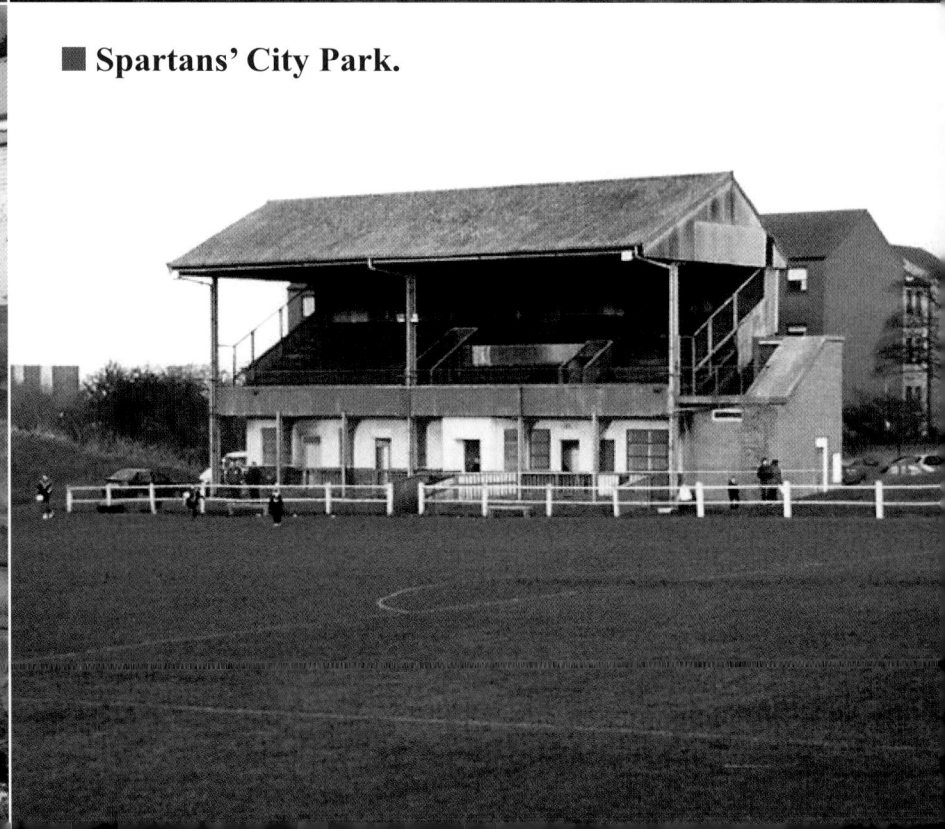

Bellshill Athletic's Brandon Park.

Whitletts Victoria's Voluntary Park.

Bankfoot Athletic's Coronation Park.

Ardrossan's Winton Park.

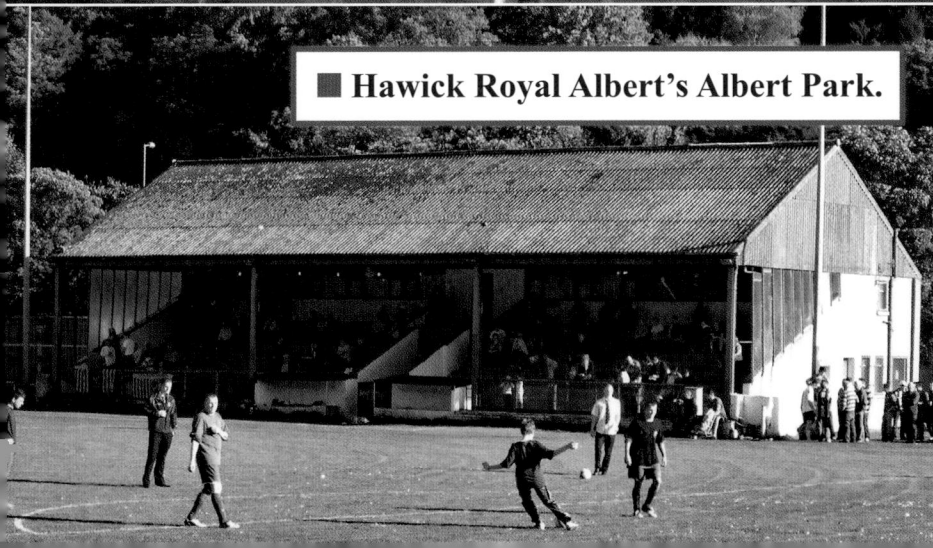
Hawick Royal Albert's Albert Park.

Tarff Rovers' Balgreen Park.

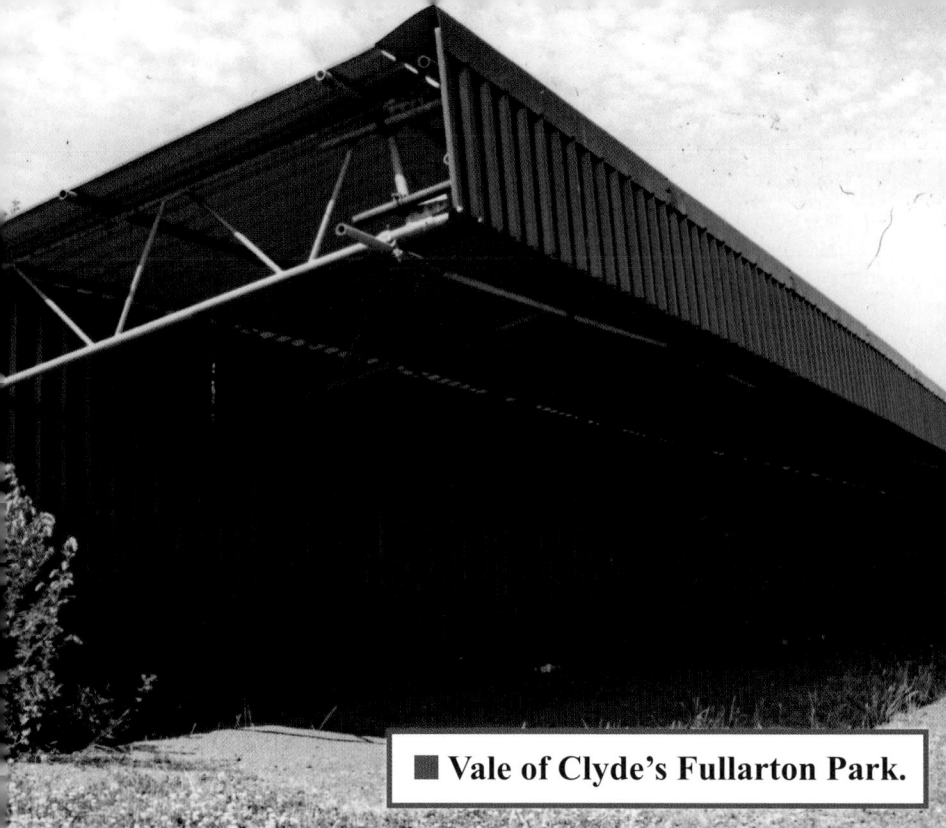

■ Vale of Clyde's Fullarton Park.

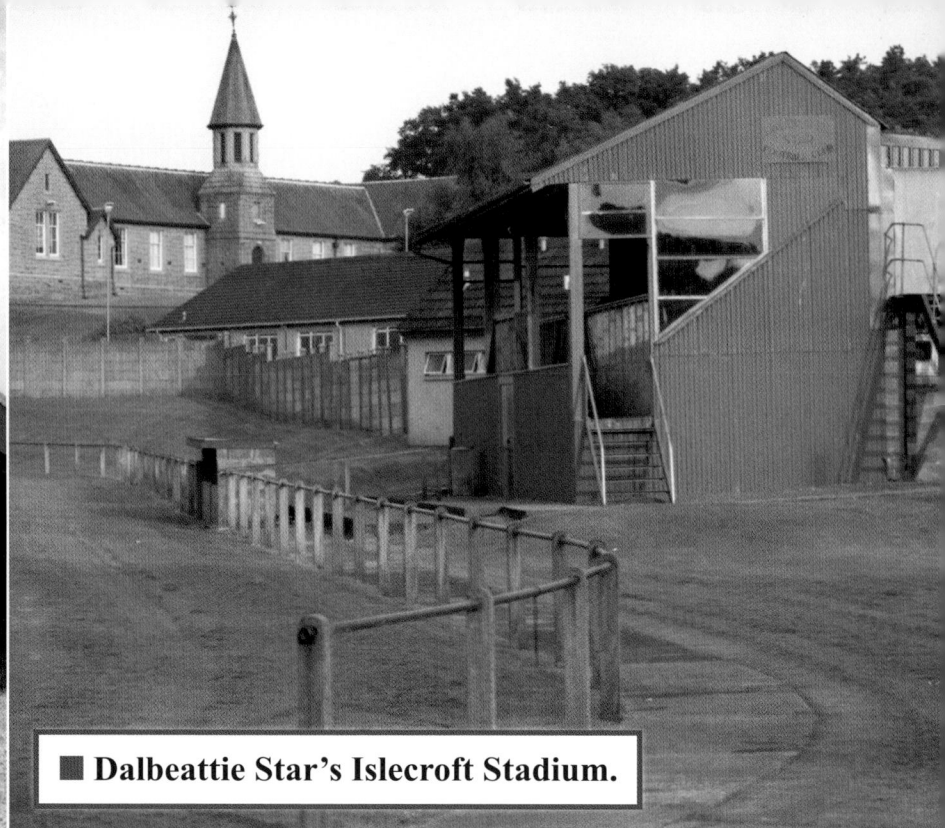

■ Dalbeattie Star's Islecroft Stadium.

■ Yoker Athletic's Holm Park.

■ Arthurlie's Dunterlie Park.

■ July 1960, St Johnstone's pre-season training at Petershill Park. The Saintees, newly-crowned Second Division champions, were a mainly part-time club at that time and drew most of their players from the west. So all but two of the squad, Ian Gardiner and Johnny Duncan, trained twice a week at the home of The Peasy.

■ Blantyre Celtic's Craighead Park.

■ Newtongrange Star's Victoria Park.

■ St Cuthbert Wanderers' St Mary's Park.

■ Armadale Thistle's Volunteer Park.

■ Camelon's Carmuirs Park.

■ Penicuik's Eastfield Park.

■ Bathgate Thistle's Creamery Park.

■ Arbroath Vics' Ogilvy Park.

■ Blairgowrie's Davie Park.

■ Forfar West End's Strathmore Park.

■ Irvine Meadow's Meadow Park.

■ Forfar Albion's Guthrie Park.

236

Shawfield Juniors' Rosebery Park.

Lossiemouth's Grant Park.

Pumpherston's Recreation Park.

■ Cambuslang Rangers' Somervell Park.

■ Renfrew FC's Western Park.

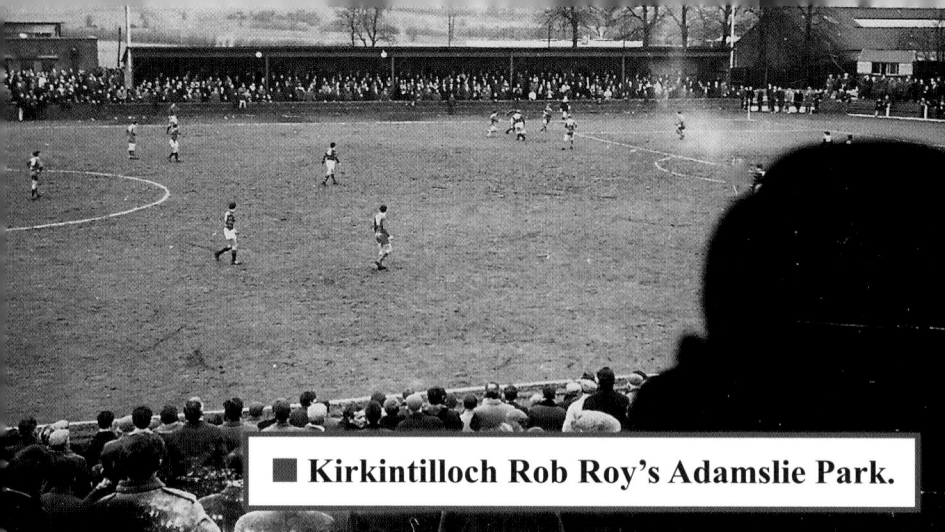

■ Kirkintilloch Rob Roy's Adamslie Park.

■ Shotts Bon Accord's Hannah Park.

■ Benburb's Tinto Park.

■ Lanark United's Moor Park.

■ Cumbernauld's Guy's Meadow.

■ Brechin Vics' Victoria Park.

■ Maryhill's Lochburn Park.

■ Saltcoats Victoria's Campbell Park.

■ Jeanfield Swifts' Simpson Park.

■ Shettleston's Greenfield Park.

■ Rutherglen Glencairn's Southcroft Park.

■ Cumnock's Townhead Park.

■ Pollok's Newlandsfield Park.

■ Girvan's Hamilton Park.

■ Troon FC's Portland Park.

■ **Fraserburgh FC's Bellslea Park, overlooked by the spire of the town's South Church. The ground welcomed Celtic on April 28th, 1970, just a week before the European Cup Final in the San Siro, Milan. Jock Stein took a full first-team squad to play a benefit for the victims of the Fraserburgh Lifeboat Disaster of January 21st, 1970. Five men had been lost when the boat overturned on its way to aid a stricken Danish trawler. More than 6,500 attended the game (played in a freezing gale-force wind) and raised £2,000.**

Motherwell

ONE of the traditionally big and successful Scottish clubs, Motherwell have played at Fir Park (named because it was set in parkland when built) since 1895.

Motherwell's biggest ever crowd came during the incredible 18-day period in early 1952 that saw four Scottish clubs welcome in their record attendances. Arbroath, Queen of the South and Airdrie, alongside Motherwell, had their biggest crowds in those few days, all in the Scottish Cup.

We will never see the likes again.

Fir Park's contribution was 35,632 against Rangers in a quarter-final replay, on March 12th. The ground held crowds of more than 30,000 on many occasions, but this was the peak.

Some estimates have suggested the crowd that day was closer to 41,000 or even 42,000 with not every spectator counted, and more gaining entry by climbing over walls.

Motherwell won 2-1, after going a goal behind, then beat Hearts in a fantastically entertaining semi that went to two replays. In the final, they thrashed Dundee 4-0 at Hampden in front of 136,495, the biggest ever crowd for a club match in Scotland that didn't involve Celtic or Rangers.

Tickets weren't issued for the game, every man jack of the crowd paid cash to get in.

■ **The distinctive round windows at the Knowetop Avenue End of Fir Park, which were demolished to make way for the Davie Cooper Stand.**

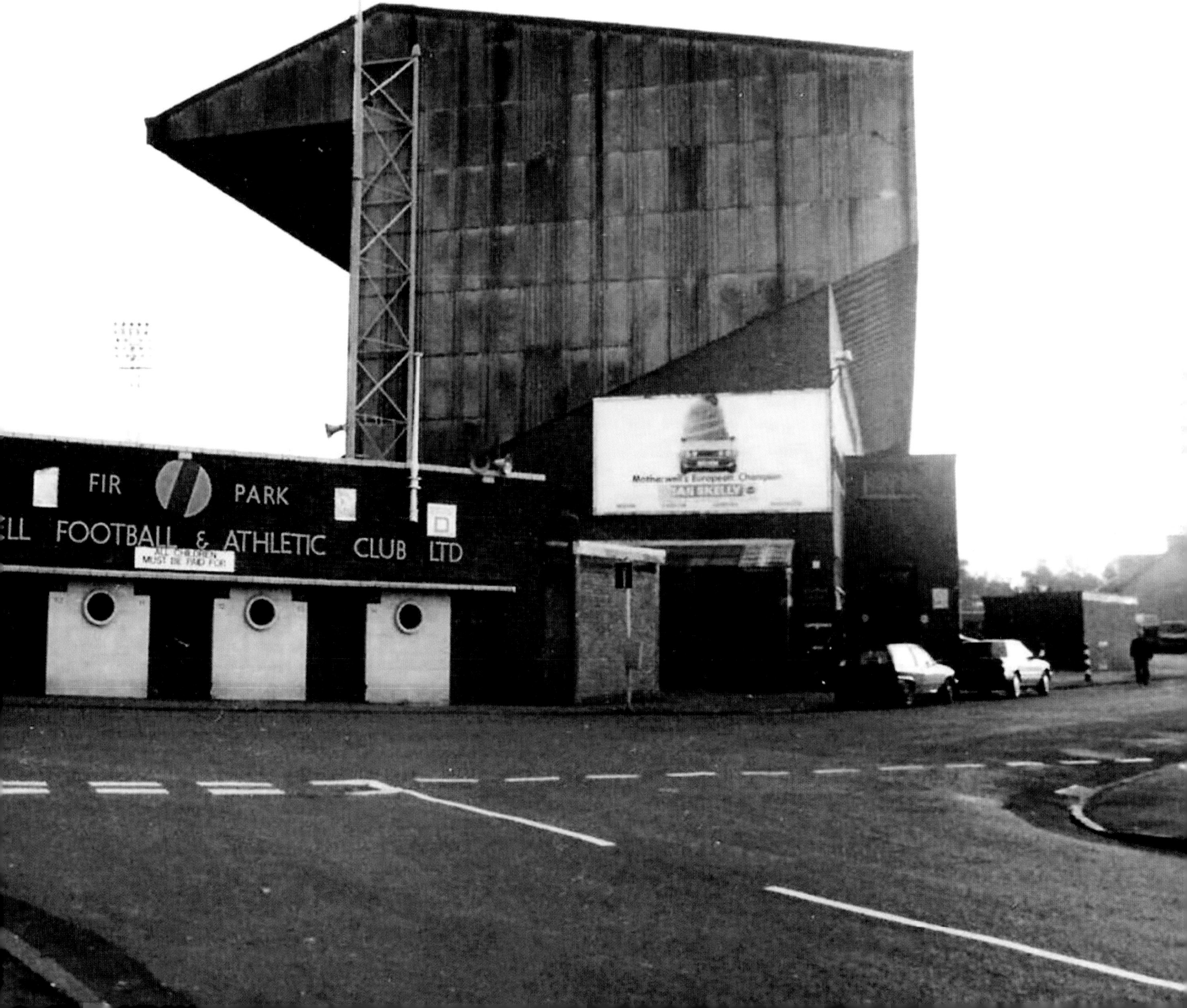

FIR PARK
ELL FOOTBALL & ATHLETIC CLUB LTD
ALL CHILDREN MUST BE PAID FOR
Motherwell's European Champion

■ Speed-demon outside-left George Lindsay displaying his keepie-up skills at the back of the old Fir Park stand. Such prominent chimneys were rare, even for a stand of this era. The photos were taken in 1961 to mark George's call-up to the Scotland Under-23 squad, with the stand about to be demolished and replaced.

246

■ **December 1951. Archie Kelly, one of the finest centre-forwards in Motherwell's history, attended by a phalanx of Aberdeen defenders led by Alec Young, in front of the old Fir Park main stand.**

■ Motherwell goalkeeper John Gardiner gives the Fir Park groundsman a hand in July 1985, in front of the new (1962) main stand.

■ 'Well's Wilson Humphries, Jackie Hunter and Charlie Cox out on the wing, in an unusual white change strip, during the 1953-54 season just before Fir Park's long side roof went up.

■ Pat Delaney, a 'Well defender of note (and superb free-kick taker) gets up highest in a match against Killie in 1964, with the by-then-covered terracing behind.

■ Andy Weir, with bandaged head, during the first leg of the Scottish Summer Cup Final v Dundee United in May 1965. 'Well won this game 3-1 and would lift the trophy 3-2 on aggregate.

The Summer Cup was played five times during the Second World War, and revived in 1964 – though without Celtic or Rangers. Jock Stein's Hibs beat Aberdeen to win it in 1964 in a final delayed two months by the typhoid outbreak which all but quarantined Aberdeen off from the rest of Scotland. The disease killed three people, affecting a further 400.

Only 11 teams entered the 1966 Summer Cup, effectively finishing the idea.

The trophy was gifted permanently to Hibs to mark chairman Harry Swan's prominent role in establishing the competition in the war years.

A full to overflowing Knowetop End on May 7th, 1966. Celtic were about to win the first of Jock Stein's nine championships.

254

The south end of Fir Park was sometimes called the Dalziel Estate End, though the 1960-61 Motherwell FC handbook calls it the Curling Pond End. This is December 18th, 1971. John Muir challenges Celtic's (formerly Motherwell's) Dixie Deans, with 'Well's Brian Heron on the left and Jackie McInally on the right. Kenny Dalglish, playing in midfield, is to the left wearing No.4. He scored two in a 5-1 Celtic win.

■ The Knowetop End (above, behind celebrated goalkeeper Hastie Weir. And right, just before being demolished in 1994). Fir Park was one of the grounds where it used to be possible for supporters to change ends at half-time. The lean-on barriers were, in Scotland's steel town, probably from a nearby foundry. There wasn't a definitive design, just an application of common sense. The shape of these barriers was likely the work of a local works foreman. The stanchions were sunk in to, or bolted to, the concrete terracing or (in the older photo) sunk into the ash. The horizontal bars were tubular. Motherwell had

an all-barriers-in-a-row layout, although there were different arrangements at other grounds. The idea was to stagger openings between the barriers, to prevent a crowd sway starting at the back of the terrace and carrying scores, even hundreds, of people down to the perimeter wall. But, again, there were no real guidelines for any of this. Most crush barriers were designed to not allow people to sit on them (or at least make it difficult) as fans behind wouldn't have been able to see. There are a few barriers here which are strengthened with extra struts – this will have been because of loosened concrete or corroded ironwork.

Dundee United

TANNADICE has changed, as Dundee United as a club has changed, in a radical manner over the past 60 years.

United struggled in the decades before and after the war. In their first 52 years of existence, 1909 to 1960, they spent just four seasons in the top division, finishing bottom of it in two of those seasons and avoiding relegation only once. They spent most of the 1930s, and all the '40s and '50s, in the lower reaches of the game – twice finishing second bottom of the Second, or B, Division.

Tannadice in those days could be described at best as "rudimentary". The terraces were grass banks until 1925 and even then were replaced mostly by old railway sleepers.

It was a battle, year after unrewarded year. But, strange to say, the supporters are now very proud of that defiant struggle. The idea of United as "Dundee's people's club" was born in this era.

The one thing United had in their favour is that they were based in one of Scotland's bigger cities. There was always support for Dundee's non-establishment club among the city's working classes. If things could improve on the pitch the crowds would come.

The catalyst was Taypools, an idea copied from Nottingham Forest by the Dundee United Sportsmen's Club. United were the first in Scotland to have their own pools competition. It was highly successful and funded the revamp of the ground.

Former player Jerry Kerr's arrival as manager in 1959 completed the set-up. His astute football brain, backed by the financial clout to bring in players – often from Scandinavia – set United, and their ground, on an upwards trajectory.

■ **The Tannadice pavilion, with its rooftop training light, prior to the 1960 stand being built. The pavilion was in the south-east corner, where the players' tunnel is now.**

'DEXTORA' THE BETTER GLUCOSE DRINK

■ The old Tannadice stand. Around 1,200 could cram on to its bench seats – if they didn't mind being rather close to their neighbour. You had to watch out if there was a vigorous celebration of a goal as forky-tailies would be shaken loose and fall on you from the roof. The tiny dugouts are in the middle, between "drink" and "replaces" on the pitch-side advertisement.

REPLACES   LOST   ENERGY   NEW - PRICE   2/6   PEF

■ A fish-eyed lens view of what Tannadice had become by 1983.

Because United were slow to become big, their biggest crowd is late too. While most Scottish clubs saw their best attendances in football's boom years of the 1930s or 1950s, the most spectators Tannadice ever hosted was for a game in the 1960s.

As any Dundee United fan will tell you (probably at great length) they are the only British club to have played the mighty Barcelona four times in European competition and beaten them four times – two home wins, two away wins.

The first of those home games, on November 16th, attracted Tannadice's record-setting crowd of 28,000.

United, with Viking imports Lennart Wing, Orjan Persson, Mogens Berg and Finn Seeman, had finished fifth in 1965-66 and qualified for the Fairs Cup, their first foray into Europe. They drew the Catalan giants in the second round after a bye in the first.

Barcelona were holders of the trophy, having beat Real Zaragoza just two months previously on September 21st – the final having been held over until after the 1966 World Cup as the Barca v Chelsea semi-final had gone to a third game.

Against all odds, United had won 2-1 in the Nou Camp three weeks beforehand on October 25th, twice hitting the home side on the break.

But Barcelona were coming to Dundee to win. They made no bones about it. Indeed they gave interviews telling how they'd do it.

Most of Europe reckoned the Scots upstarts had had their day, and would now be shown what was what by an elite club.

Unfortunately, the Barcelona players believed the hype and played almost without urgency, as if it were them who held a first-leg lead. The United players went at them like The Terrors that is the club's nickname, and won, entirely deservedly, 2-0 for a 4-1 aggregate amid incredible scenes of celebration on the steep Tannadice slopes.

United had the ball in the net on two other occasions that night and were also denied what looked a stonewall penalty.

The Dundee public had eagerly queued to buy the 28,000 tickets and more could, and probably should, have been sold. United, like many clubs in those unregulated days, had no clear idea of how many spectators their ground could hold. They'd never had such an attendance. It was admitted years later that the decision to print 28,000 tickets had been little more than an educated guess.

In the next round, which wasn't until the new year, United drew another European giant, Juventus.

Again they were away from home in the first leg. But the Italians, who would be Serie A champions that season, weren't as complacent as the Spanish had been and won 3-0.

In front of their second highest attendance of all time, 27,245, United won the second leg 1-0 on March 8th, 1967, to restore some Scottish pride.

United, that season, were also the only team to do a league double (both times by a score of 3-2) over European Cup and domestic treble-winning Celtic.

■ Left: United captain Jimmy Briggs shakes hands with Barcelona skipper Lucien Muller-Schmidt.

■ **Above: Dundee United v Juventus, March 8th, 1967. The second biggest crowd Tannadice has ever seen.**

■ **Left: Dundee United v Barcelona, November 16th, 1966. Belgian referee Robert Schaut appears to have spotted his Uncle Boab in the tight-packed crowd.**

■ The pic above is the north terracing at Tannadice, pictured on a dreich Dundee day in January 1957, before it was restructured. It was a lower terrace in those days. The photo on the right was taken on July 11th, 1962, and shows the moulds for concrete to be poured for the new terrace. The "risers" (as builders call them – better known as steps to most of us) for the new terrace were eight inches. The usual riser height in Scottish grounds was three or four, sometimes as little as two, inches. It was these unusually high steps that

gave "the cliff" at Tannadice such a steep angle. Note that the Tannadice pitch has moved about ten yards to the north (there is a clear line in the grass). This was in part to accommodate the new, deeper stand on the other side of the ground, though the formerly tight playing surface was also widened. The effects of this repositioning are still apparent today. "The Shed", built in 1957, was aligned to the old pitch. Since the pitch moved, the roof is too long on its south side and doesn't quite reach the shy line of the pitch on its north side.

"It's Grand Beer" Drybroughs

Legend has it that Dundee United fans are nicknamed "The Arabs" because of a match on a frozen Tannadice pitch in 1963.

The story goes that United burned off the ice with braziers and tar-laying equipment, but also burned off the grass. They then spread tons of sand on the surface.

United won 3-0 and played so well that a newspaper report (in the less politically-sensitive manner of those times) said they "took to the sand like Arabs".

And the name stuck.

It's a nice, indeed romantic, tale and many United supporters swear it is true. But it isn't.

United did melt the ice to get that game on, but despite an exhaustive search of newspaper databases, microfiche pages, dusty archives, and the recollections of hacks in the newspaper trade at the time – indeed some who were in the Tannadice press box that very day – there is no mention of United as "Arabs" in any newspaper that year, or for several years afterwards.

In any case, it was the fans who became known as Arabs, not the team.

The true story isn't so neat and tidy, and requires a short history lesson.

Gamal Abdel Nasser was the de facto leader of the Arab world from his election as president of Egypt in 1956 and throughout the 1960s. He was a giant of Middle Eastern politics. He defied the West during the Suez Crisis and became the figurehead of

▪ Left: the strenuous efforts to get Tannadice playable in time for the Scottish Cup tie against Albion Rovers on January 26th, 1963. This was the so-called "Arabs" game.

pan-Arabism, the push to unite all Arab nations. He inspired devotion from his followers and fear in oil-hungry world countries in equal measure. He was an inspirational speechmaker and to this day is regarded, by some, as an icon, a strong man who brought leadership to an often difficult region.

He was famous in the 1960s, even in Dundee.

In Tannadice's Amalfi End, named for a chip shop near the east end of the ground, there would be, at every game, a thinnish, middle-aged man wearing a long overcoat and a bunnet.

Inspired by Liverpool's Kop, football crowds had begun singing pop songs with changed lyrics to suit their team, or celebrate their star players.

Led by that cheerleader in the bunnet, Dundee United fans were no different.

He would stand amid a couple of hundred of his "choirboys" and shout: 'T-E-R-R-O-R-S, are we the Terrors?' – 'YES, YES, YES', would come the reply from his boys. Like every set of supporters at the time, more songs would flow.

This type of singing and chanting hadn't really been done in football grounds before the 1960s. The hymn *Abide With Me* had long been sung before bigger games, and there was sometimes community singing of hymns and popular songs – but this idea of supporters independently inventing songs was new.

Younger fans, of all clubs, loved it.

At Tannadice one day, the bunneted man bellowed: "I AM NASSER AND YOU ARE MY ARABS!"

His boys liked this name for "their gang" and United supporters have been "Arabs" ever since, though many of them have forgotten why.

■ The long-gone Tannadice Souvenir Shop that used to be perched, a little strangely, half-way up the stairs under the main stand.

Many Arabs over the age of about 50 will spent time in a queue on those cold concrete steps to buy match tickets, programmes or enamel badges from this tiny shop.

The shop, now renamed, has premises in the concourses behind the 1990s George Fox and Eddie Thomson stands.

■ The Tannadice undersoil heating being installed in June 1985. A pitch heating system was, much like when floodlights began to be installed, a matter of snobbery for football fans. If your club's ground had heated grass, but your rivals didn't, it was a chance to look down your nose at the old-fashioned quaintness of "them" who hadn't yet moved up to this new level. This photo, if nothing else, reveals what a 1980s undersoil heating system actually looked like.

Not just football

A FOOTBALL ground is used for first-team games on perhaps 20 occasions a year. The other 345 days it stands empty.

And it costs small fortunes to buy the land, build and maintain grounds, and keep them up to date with safety legislation.

To earn desperately needed extra revenue they have been put to many other uses over the years.

Some predictable, some not.

■ **This photo shows speedway racing, Great Britain v Sweden, at Albion Rovers' Cliftonhill in 1968, with spectators turning away from the cast-up grit.**

Speedway was also staged at Celtic Park in 1928; Hampden 1969-72; Shawfield 1988-98; Cowdenbeath in 1965; Meadowbank until 1967; and still goes on at Shielfield Park, home track of Berwick Bandits since 1968.

Dog racing was a common alternative use of grounds.

Firhill, Celtic Park, Love Street, Dens Park, Muirton, Cliftonhill, Bayview, Cappielow, Boghead, Brockville, Tannadice, Firs Park, East End Park, Shielfield Park and Central Park all hosted dog racing at some point.

But making money was another story. Dog racing needed significant alterations to grounds, with many more ongoing costs.

Dundee spent £800,000 on a track in the 1990s, but never made a penny. Unluckily, the Dens dogs launched at the same time as evening horse racing began to be screened live in bookies' premises.

■ Left: Shawfield – a dog track that happened to have a football pitch. Willie McLean, the former Motherwell manager, spent the 1963-64 season as a Clyde player. He recalled that you had to be prepared for a pungent surprise if you tried a sliding tackle where the dogs were walked between races!

■ Right: Greyhounds paraded on the Dens track in 1994.

■ An atmospheric shot of the ill-fated Dundee FC greyhounds experiment in 1994. There had also been dog racing at Dens between 1932 and 1936.

1954. The Duke of Edinburgh uses the Ibrox pitch as a parking place, then says how-de-do to Rangers boss Scot Symon. He was joining his wife on a tour of Scotland to celebrate her accession to the throne.

■ To the skirl of the pipes, a display of Scottish Country Dancing at half-time during the Scotland v Denmark match of May 12th, 1951. The game was part of the Festival of Britain. Scotland won 3-1 on a very warm day in Glasgow, and lined up: Cowan (Morton), Young (Rangers, captain), Cox (Rangers), Scoular (Portsmouth), Woodburn (Rangers), Redpath (Motherwell), Waddell (Rangers), Johnstone (Hibernian), Reilly (Hibernian), Steel (Dundee), Mitchell (Newcastle United). Reserves were: Mason (Third Lanark), McNaught (Raith Rovers), Hamilton (Aberdeen), McColl (Rangers).

282

■ American evangelist Billy Graham was famous in the 1950s and '60s for his "crusades". He undertook a quite remarkable 417 of these in 185 countries between 1947 and 2005. The crowds he drew were also remarkable, topped by a 1.1 million-strong rally in Seoul, South Korea, in 1973. He didn't attract quite that number to Ibrox. There had been 100,000 tickets available, but the attendance on Saturday, June 24th, 1961, was about 37,000 – still impressive. Dr Graham addressed those present, warning them that

the world had become obsessed with sex. He specifically condemned "back seat immorality in cars" and the prevalence of "heavy petting in parks". He promised that such depravity would "destroy your souls". Note the temporary passageways put in place to allow spectators easy access to go on to the pitch, should they be moved by the spirit to do so. Football spectators filled with spirits were never encouraged to make their way on to the field of play.

■ Cowdenbeath's Central Park has hosted stock car racing and dog racing, but in the mid-1960s grown men relived their childhoods with gird and cleek racing round the track. Takes a bit of skill, y'know.

Kirkcaldy Highland Games were held at Raith Rovers' Stark's Park for several years. These grainy photos are from 1925.

No one could say the obstacle race wasn't made interesting. The bottom pic is the dash (sprint) about to start.

Highland Games nowadays are fun family outings. It was different in the 1920s. Quite substantial sums could be won all around Scotland, and men ran hard because it was a way to put bread on the table. It might be their only way to do so.

A victor's name would be communicated to the next week's venue and a handicap of several yards was applied so the race was as tough – as cut-throat – as possible.

■ **Perhaps the most surprising, indeed startling, alternative use for a football ground was this ski jump, erected at Wembley in May 1961.**

The slope was an aluminium scaffolding construction 150 feet high. It had wooden boards, with straw scattered over them to stop the snow sliding off. Around 50 tons of "snow" (really crushed ice) was used but it had to be continually topped up in the warm weather.

Impressively, the whole structure – which was 376 feet long – took only 36 hours to build. An international field of jumpers was assembled, including all the great names of the day from France, West Germany and the Nordic countries.

Various "fun" jumps were also made, including one by a man dressed as a London City gent in a bowler hat, and a Viking with a horned helmet. All of them were, however, Scandinavian experts.

Swiftly erected ski jumps were fairly common in towns across the USA in the 1930s, where they seem to have been regarded much like travelling circuses.

The Rangers Annual Sports, held at the start of August each year, was probably the most famous, most successful, and longest running alternative use for a Scottish football stadium.

Revered Rangers manager Bill Struth had been a professional runner himself before his career in football. He was the driving force behind the Sports for many years and would travel to London, even New York, to sign up the greatest athletes of the day.

Crowds of 50,000 and 60,000 were common, with the 1947 Sports drawing 70,000. This was attractive to athletes who rarely performed before such numbers even at Olympic Games.

The Sports started as far back as the 1880s, with the last meeting being 1962.

The names who took part included some of the greatest of all time. Paavo Nurmi, the "Flying Finn" who set 22 world records over the course of his career, ran at the 1931 Sports. Hurdler Don Finlay, Spitfire ace and Olympic team captain, was there in 1948.

Sports were also held at Hampden. Runner and pentathlete Fanny Blankers-Koen (see next page) who won four golds at the 1948 London Olympics was treated like a Hollywood star when she attended.

■ **Left: the pole vault, in the 1950s, had athletes landing on piles of sand, not pads.**

■ **Right: A vast crowd cheers the long jump.**

■ Above: Ibrox high jump – the Fosbury Flop didn't become the dominant jumping technique until 1968.

■ Right: Superstar Fanny Blankers-Koen (with pockets on her tracksuit) and British Olympic sprinter June Faulds were the centre of attention at the Hampden Police Sports of 1952, before another big crowd.

■ **Left: American middle-distance superstar Tom Courtney, who would go on to take two gold medals at the 1956 Olympics in Melbourne, wins the half-mile at Ibrox in 1955.**

■ **Right: Rangers manager Scot Symon asks Courtney if he might be able to play on the left wing.**

Raith Rovers

ALTHOUGH a figure of 31,306 for a 1953 game against Hearts is usually claimed as the biggest ever Stark's Park crowd, it is actually 32,867 for an earlier cup-tie, against Hibs, on January 26, 1952.

There is quite a story to that crowd.

The police insisted on a 30,000 capacity, despite the club claiming 36,000 could be accommodated. Legendary Raith manager Bert Herdman had more tickets printed incrementally as additional railway sleepers were laid near the top of the ash banking terracing. Then he rolled out even more trackside seating.

The town council were praised for providing workers to clear the pitch of snow (for the third time in 24 hours) to allow the game to proceed, and for hauling in the new seating for around the pitch.

This was double-tiered. Adults were charged 3/- for an individual chair, children were admitted to sit on benches in front of them.

By the time all these "extras" were added, the final figure was the aforementioned 32,867 – more than likely without Fife's chief constable ever knowing.

And they saw a cracking game. Rovers blunted the Famous Five attack (Hibs were League champions that season) and had the best of the chances, though it finished 0-0. The replay was also 0-0 then Rovers won the second replay, at Tynecastle, 4-1.

■ **Rovers' record appearance-maker Willie McNaught (657 games between 1941 and 1962) at Stark's Park in 1957.**

Jimmy (as he was known in his Rovers days) Baxter, aged 20, in December 1959.

■ **March 8th, 1969, looking towards the south end of Stark's Park. A crowd of 16,000 saw Rovers take a 1-0 lead (Gordon Wallace) just after half-time, but Celtic fought back to win 3-1 (Willie Wallace 2, Bertie Auld). The dejection of Rovers defenders Ken McDonald (No. 2) and Willie Polland (No. 5) is clear to see.**

■ Rovers keeper Charlie Drummond beats Hibs' Joe Baker to the ball. It is November 14th, 1959, a league game that Rovers won 4-2. The Stark's Park coo shed, or railway stand, is on the left.

■ A decent crowd, swelled by a good travelling support, inside the Meadowbank Stadium for the visit of Inverness Caley on January 28th, 1978. The angle of this pic doesn't properly illustrate the distance between the one stand (also pictured, right) and the pitch. Billy Urquhart is shown getting Caley's goal in a 2-1 win for Meadowbank in the third round of the Scottish Cup. Billy moved to Rangers later in 1978 – John Greig's first signing as a manager – then played for Wigan Athletic, but returned north to become a Caley legend. He played 688 games and scored 393 goals over his two spells, before retiring in 1993.

Ferranti Thistle, Meadowbank, Livingston

IT'S been a long road to Almondvale for the club that is now Livingston FC.

Works team Ferranti Thistle (Ferranti was an electrical engineering firm) formed in 1943, became Meadowbank Thistle and were admitted to the league in 1974. Then in 1995 Meadowbank became Livingston FC and relocated 20 miles to West Lothian.

Almondvale is too new for this book, but the Meadowbank Stadium, built for the 1970 Commonwealth Games, qualifies as a Scottish football stadium of the black & white era.

When Meadowbank Thistle played there it was criticised for having just the one stand and for the pitch being far away across the running track. This didn't help foster a traditional football stadium-type atmosphere.

The stand had a notional 7,000 capacity. With the stadium's surrounding bench seating, 16,000 could get in for athletics meetings. But football attendances were limited to 3,500.

Largely unloved as a "real" fitba venue the stand was demolished and the ground rebuilt, with a 500 capacity, for Edinburgh City FC.

Inverness

IT is a constant annoyance to supporters of smaller clubs that patronising suggestions of amalgamation keep coming down from the upper reaches of the game.

The ideas are for one bigger club in, for instance, Dundee to replace Dundee FC and Dundee United. Or Falkirk to replace Falkirk FC and East Stirlingshire. Or, they used to say, between the three Highland League teams in Inverness.

Supporters of smaller clubs are passionate about their team and history and love their ground as much as any other fan. It might sound logical to an accountant, but the amalgamation of football clubs is very unusual.

Yet it happened in Inverness in 1994.

Clachnacuddin stayed out of it, but Caledonian and Thistle merged to form one club that would join the Scottish league system. To some supporters (though not all) the amalgamation is, to this day, a cause of angst.

This chapter celebrates the history and grounds of all three Inverness clubs, as they used to be.

Thistle played at Kingsmills Park between 1895 and 1994.

Caledonian played at Telford Street Park between 1926 and 1996 (the merged club initially also played at Telford Street before the move to their current home, Caledonian Stadium).

Clachnacuddin play at Grant Street Park, as they have done since 1886.

■ **Right: Caledonian's Telford Street Park in 1988.**

■ Thistle's Kingsmills Park in March 1995, after the club had moved out to take part in the merger the previous year. The photo on the right, over the wall, shows the sad sight of the old place neglected and overgrown. That year, 1995, was the 100-year anniversary of Kingsmills' first Thistle game.

■ Kingsmills had one of the best playing surfaces in the Highlands and was often used for Highland cup finals and select games. The 600-seat stand shown here was built in 1951, following several years without a stand as the original wooden one had burned down at the start of the Second World War. The ground was used as a military camp during that conflict. Shortly after this photo was taken, the area was developed into residential properties and a nursing home. The floodlights had already been sold to Wick Academy FC.

■ Clach's Grant Street Park in 1969, when it had turf slopes behind the goal.

A major fire in 1988, destroyed the old wooden stand shown here with the writing on the roof.

The "Ferry San Siro" now has a capacity of 2,074.

■ **May 23rd, 1988. Firefighters rush to tackle the fire that devastated Clach's Grant Street Park.**

■ October 20th, 1996. The players are piped out the tunnel for the last ever game at Telford Street. Inverness Caledonian Thistle's opposition were a Highland League select, who won 3-0. ICT moved to the purpose-built 7,512-capacity Tulloch Stadium, which was later renamed the Caledonian Stadium.

310

There is debate over the biggest ever football crowd in Inverness. Do only competitive games count?

A Caley and Thistle select welcomed Celtic (Jock Stein bringing the full first team) on May 11th, 1968, to play a benefit for the dependents of Andy "Jupie" Mitchell, a famous Highland footballer who had died at the tragically young age of 39.

That game drew a 10,000 all-ticket crowd to Telford Street.

Kingsmills had 7,550 on February 21st, 1972, when Celtic again came to town to inaugurate Thistle's floodlights.

There were around 9,000 at Grant Street to see Rangers play a benefit for Bobby Bolt (who had played for the Ibrox club in the 1940s) on August 22nd, 1951. But it was Caley they played as the new stand at Telford Street wasn't complete.

Rangers came north again on April 5th, 1952, to play an Inverness Select, again at Grant Street. This time playing to an estimated 7,500.

■ **Left: The queue for tickets to a Scottish Cup Fourth Round tie, a competitive game, at Telford Street in February 1984. Rangers beat Caley 6-0 in front of an all-ticket 5,500.**

Berwick
Rangers

■ The Rangers of Berwick and Glasgow seem to be intertwined. The biggest crowd at Shielfield Park came on January 30th, 1960, when a 9000-strong travelling support swelled the attendance to 16,000. Glasgow Rangers won that cup-tie 3-1. The famous 1-0 Scottish Cup win for the home side in 1967 drew 13,283. The game pictured here, another cup-tie, on January 28th, 1978, was a 4-2 victory for Glasgow Rangers, but only drew a crowd of 10,500, though the terraces look full to bursting.

The short shed on the west side of Shielfield, shown on the previous page, is the Ducket (dovecote), while the long, low roof on this page is the main stand.

The Wee Rangers man in this photo (being challenged by John Greig) is Ian Smith, who scored one of Berwick's goals in the 1978 4-2 game.

Ian is a stalwart of the club. He started at Dundee and had spells at Alloa and Meadowbank but played much of his career at Berwick. He became a coach, then later a director for a time.

He was followed to Shielfield by his son Darren, who had a lengthy career at the other Rangers in Glasgow, then Brechin City, Raith Rovers, Alloa, East Fife and Arbroath, before returning to Berwick as player-coach.

Cowdenbeath

CENTRAL PARK'S biggest ever crowd was the culmination of what was a quite sensational story in post-war Scottish football.

'Beath had been dealt a hard hand by events surrounding the war. They had won the 1938-39 B Division and were playing top-flight football (as they had done for much of the inter-war years) when the leagues were abandoned after five games in the autumn of 1939.

When the leagues were re-formed after hostilities, the Fife club was placed back into the B Division.

They didn't fare too well in the immediate post-war years, but made it to the two-legged quarter-final of the League Cup in 1949. They were to play Rangers, who had already beaten Celtic, Aberdeen and St Mirren in the competition.

The first leg was incredible. Cowdenbeath recorded a 3-2 victory, the first time Rangers had ever been beaten at home by a lower division club.

This set all Fife abuzz. There was massive interest in the second leg to take place just four days later.

A crowd of 25,586 somehow got in to Central Park on the evening of Wednesday, September 21st, 1949.

Cowdenbeath got off to a great start and were a goal up at half-time, putting them two ahead of Rangers on aggregate.

But Rangers, as club tradition demands, fought back and scored two in the second half, though the second goal went in with just 15 seconds left. This put the aggregate score at 4-4 and sent the tie into extra-time.

The Glasgow giants scored after 12 minutes of the extra period to make it 5-4, but the game remained close right to the very end – which in those days before floodlights meant high drama in the gathering darkness.

Central Park's main stand was built in 1922, and most of it remains to this day. It was, when first opened, 120 yards long, with 14 rows of seats, and could seat 3,500. It was the pride of the club, with its centre (with dressing rooms below), east (boardroom below) and west (referee's room below) sections.

It suffered a fire in 1992 but much of the central and west sections remain. An adjoining new stand was opened in 1995.

St Johnstone's Muirton Park main stand (built in 1924) was modelled on Central Park's stand.

■ **What is Dundee full-back Bobby Wilson (though he was also an ex-Cowdenbeath star) doing at Central Park in the summer of 1970? See page 320.**

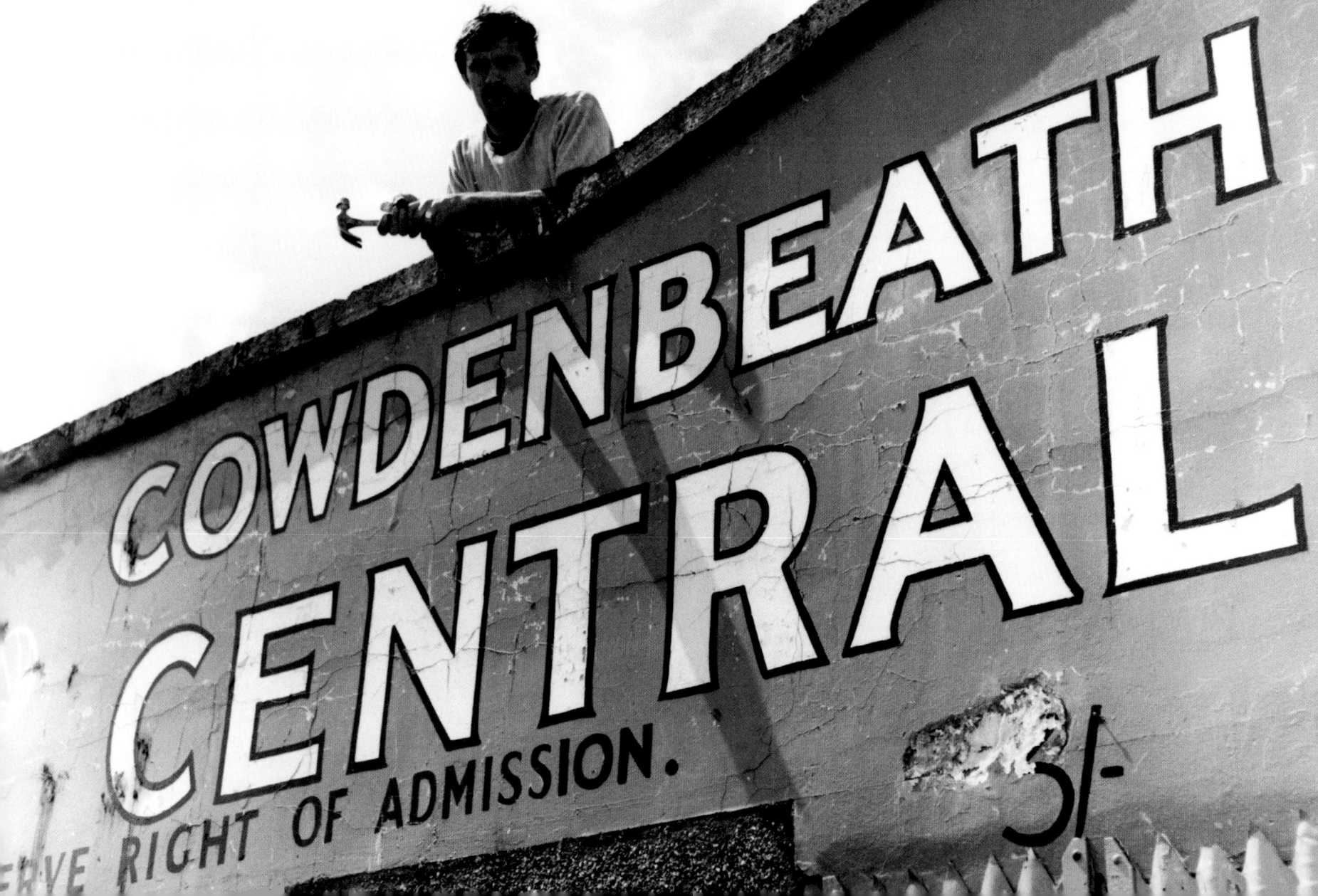

COWDENBEATH
CENTRAL

...RVE RIGHT OF ADMISSION.

3/-

In 1957, the newly-formed Cowdenbeath Football Supporters Association declared a covered enclosure would be erected at the Chapel Street end of Central Park. Voluntary labour would be used to build the structure, which was to be 75 yards long and would provide cover for 2,000 fans.

The ground was opened Monday to Friday for people to come along and help.

This was to become the famous "Cooshed" and it was ready by February 1958 for the Scottish Cup visit of Rangers.

This photo shows the Cooshed in March 1971 during Cowden's only post-war top-flight season. Billy Bostock gave the Fifers a 4th-minute lead over Celtic, but the home side eventually lost 5-1.

Bobby Lennox is shown getting a shot away.

Cowdenbeath won promotion in 1969-70 and faced a race to get the ground ready for its first top-flight season in 30 years.

Their former full-back Bobby Wilson, bought by Dundee four years previously, was a joiner to trade. In that close-season he undertook voluntary work for his old club.

Bobby put in four turnstiles that Cowdenbeath got from the by then going-to-ruin Cathkin Park (it had been three years since Third Lanark's demise).

'Beath had also considered purchasing Thirds' enclosure roof.

All the hard work paid off, with Central Park looking at its very best to welcome their first visitors of the season on August 29th, 1970 – Bobby's Dundee team who won 1-0.

Kilmarnock

RUGBY PARK was, in the days of standing crowds, a huge place. Even today, with a capacity of 18,128, it is the biggest ground outside Glasgow, Edinburgh and Aberdeen.

Like St Mirren's Love Street it was a big playing area, circled by a huge sweep of curved terraces to fit spectators on to.

The most that ever crammed in was an all-ticket 35,995 for a Scottish Cup tie against Rangers in March 1962. The club, under Willie Waddell, were emerging as a force to be reckoned with in the early 1960s and had high hopes they could see off the Ibrox men. The home crowd came out in great numbers.

On a windy day in Ayrshire it was 2-2, Killie coming back to level twice, until late McMillan and Brand goals saw Rangers through 4-2 in a thriller. The Ibrox side were on their way to winning the cup that year.

■ **This photo shows the old main stand with its barrel roof and arched middle gable. It was built in 1899 and survived for more than 60 years. The keeper is Aberdeen's Fred Martin, on December 17th, 1955. Killie won 1-0.**

324

■ **A new main stand was completed in time for the 1961-62 season and had a significantly higher capacity than the old one.**

This is the League Cup sectional game against Rangers on August 17th, 1963, which attracted another huge crowd, 34,246, almost breaking the record of the previous year.

It was an exciting time to be a Killie fan.

In the seven seasons starting from 1959-60 their league finishes were: 2nd, 2nd, 5th, 2nd, 2nd, champions, 3rd.

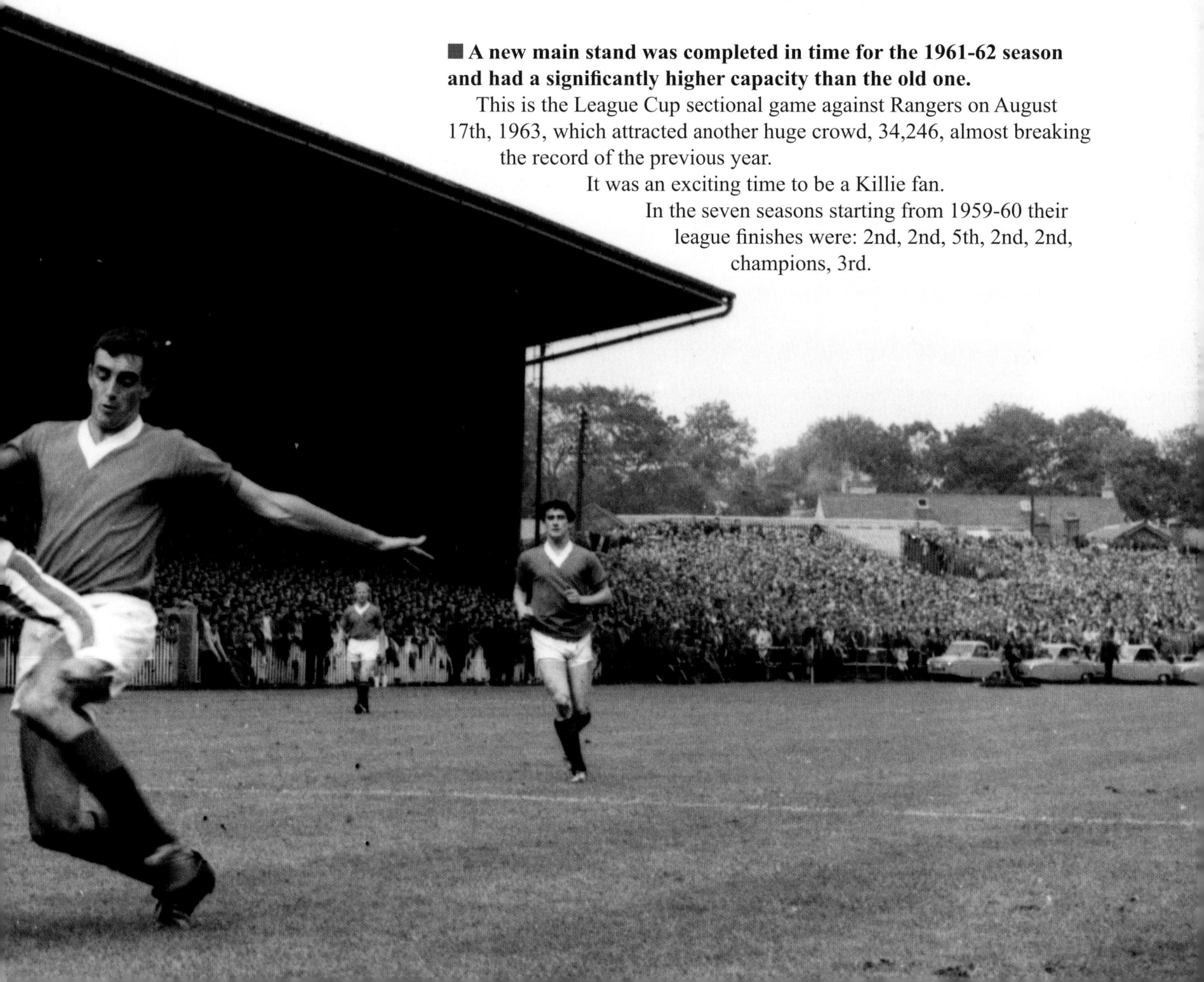

■ When full, what an atmosphere was generated at Rugby Park. This was thanks in large part to the huge East Enclosure, given a roof in 1958, which poured noise across the pitch. The photo on the left shows it full to overflowing for the visit of Rangers on February 11th, 1967. On this page, Frank Beattie and the rest of the Killie heroes show off the league trophy to that vast terrace after being crowned champions in 1964-65.

■ The south terrace's "Johnnie Walker roof", with Wolves midfielder Ron Flowers and Middlesbrough trainer Harold Shepherdson.

■ Bobby Charlton and Jimmy Greaves in front of the Stand Enclosure. The England squad were training on Rugby Park's renowned surface ahead of the 1962 Auld Enemy game.

Kilmarnock had three sheep as mascots over the middle years of the 20th Century: Ruby, Angus, and Wilma.

These photos show manager Malky MacDonald in the mid-1950s with a youthful Wilma, who lived a fine life having the run of the ground (except on match days) and died in 1966.

The story goes that the first mascot, Ruby, was one of twins, but was so weak at birth her owner gave the poor wee lamb to the son of Hughie Spence, who was manager from 1919 to 1937.

Hughie had the club trainer revive Ruby with a tot of whisky – and she became the club's sheep.

After the Scottish Cup was won for a second time in 1929 the tradition of this Killie lucky mascot was retained for decades.

A friendly at Rugby Park between Killie and Bangu AC of Brazil in 1961, in front of a crowd of 18,166. Willie Waddell's side won 1-0.

Bangu were wearing red-and-white stripes, while Killie played in all-blue.

There was an amusing incident early in the second half, when the Rio de Janeiro side put on a substitute, but didn't take anybody off (the idea of subs was virtually unknown in Scottish football at the time). Willie Waddell informed ref Willie Brittle, who counted them and told the one who had entered play to go back to the dugout.

Killie had played Bangu in the final of the inaugural New York International Tournament in the summer of 1960. On the way to that final Killie beat Bayern Munich 3-1, Irish League Champions Glenavon 2-0, English Champions Burnley 2-0, New York Americans 3-1, and drew 1-1 with OGC Nice.

This game, one of the last in front of Rugby Park's old stand, was played on April 17th, 1961.

Not far away in Irvine, that very same day, Killie's cup-winning captain of 1997, Ray Montgomerie, was being born.

Segregation

BEFORE the world became a nastier, more violent, less respectful place, segregation wasn't needed in football grounds. No one even thought of putting supporters into separate parts of the ground and fencing them off from each other.

Most walls, railings, or other measures that existed were intended to separate cheaper parts of the stadium from more expensive (usually with a roof) areas.

So Scottish football grounds weren't designed with the notion of keeping fans apart.

But when the trouble got too bad, and it did, they had to find a way.

Some put up frail fences, others (especially in the 1970s) relied on lines of policemen keeping groups of supporters at bay, with a no-man's-land in the middle.

When grounds were full, and real (or imagined) on-field injustices were whipping fans to a frenzy, the push and shove of the crowd narrowed these spaces, and the thin blue lines holding back the tide might break entirely.

It was a very unsatisfactory situation, not least for the coppers who stood between gangs of alcohol-fuelled thugs intent on getting to "the enemy" with their bovver boots.

Eventually, fences and walls were concreted into place, or clubs rearranged their inside and outside access to put crowds in completely cordoned-off stands and terraces. But this took years in some cases.

With a sometimes narrow divide between groups of fans, the throwing of missiles was common. Several grounds erected fences that stretched from terracing steps to shed roof in an attempt to combat this.

You will hear tales (and many remember) when at the smaller grounds in Scotland a good proportion of the crowd would change ends at half-time so they could stand behind the goal their team was shooting towards. Though it wasn't possible to do this at all grounds, and especially not at the Glasgow giants.

It is, however, another part of being a spectator that has disappeared from the game with the coming of all-seater stadiums. Segregation fences first made it impossible, though.

With the rise of football violence, the prospect of tribes of fans switching ends at half-time, and meeting somewhere in the middle or on walkways behind the terraces, became a flashpoint that was very difficult to police. Some of the worst confrontations within football grounds came at these points.

■ **May 11th, 1985. Hearts fans direct their chants over the Love Street segregation divide.**

336

■ No-man's-land.

The police-patrolled (with dogs) divide in the crowd for a Dundee United v Celtic game at Tannadice on November 29th, 1975.

Celtic won 3-1 in front of a crowd of 11,846.

It doesn't look too dangerous in this photo, but some games were less contentious than others, and some crowds were more difficult to control than others.

September 1975. A sign directs fans where to stand. The "home" and "away" areas at Dens Park were, in later years, switched.

DUNDEE

RANGERS

■ **October 20th, 1979. Morton, enjoying a great season orchestrated by the outrageously talented Andy Ritchie, beat Celtic 1-0 at Cappielow to go one point behind them at the top of the Premier League. It was an 18,000 all-ticket crowd. Football is a game of passions, that's why we love it. Sometimes passion spills over into confrontation – this is Morton's Davie Hayes exchanging pleasantries with Bobby Lennox. These flashpoints heighten the chance of trouble off the pitch, with supporters narrowly separated by flimsy fences.**

■ April 13th, 1985. There was a double segregation fence, with a space between, at Tynecastle. Hearts, understandably, kept the covered terracing for their own supporters. Away fans got wet. This game, however, was a Scottish Cup Semi-Final between Dundee United and Aberdeen. It was a 0-0 draw attended by 18,485. The replay, the following Wednesday, was won 2-1 by United in front of 10,771.

■ May 3rd, 1980. Hibs 0, Aberdeen 5. With such a vast terracing to utilise, Easter Road was able to put a substantial segregation divide between rival fans. This was a red letter day for Aberdeen. Their support flooded to Edinburgh and packed the Dunbar End to see Alex Ferguson's side win the title (technically they still had a game to play, but would have had to lose 10-0 to Partick). Fergie and his players celebrated at length on the pitch.

■ Sorry, another photo that will require your book to be turned on its side. And another Easter Road photo. This is Hibs v Rangers, on August 19th, 1978. An impromptu segregation divide has opened up on the vast East Terrace. This was an especially keenly-fought game on the pitch – Eddie Turnbull's Hibs battling out a 0-0 draw with John Greig's Rangers. And the hard-man stuff spread to the terraces.

This resulted in the scene you see in this slightly blurred photo, one that is virtually unknown in modern-day football stadiums. The police have identified a troublemaker and sent in a snatch team to arrest him.

To locate and then manhandle the arrested man down to the track was never an easy manoeuvre in those days when there was so much movement in the crowd, and so many hot-headed young men intent on violence. A good proportion of them were tanked up with alcohol and armed with bottles that would make effective weapons or missiles. There was always the possibility they might mount a "rescue" attempt to free their mate.

344

■ **Motherwell v Celtic, August 26th, 1978.** Fir Park had full-height anti-missile fencing. Although the point of any type of segregation divide was lost if there were Celtic supporters on both sides of it celebrating Roy Aitken's second goal in a 5-1 away win. This match was the only time brothers David Latchford (Motherwell) and Peter Latchford (Celtic) ever faced each other as professional goalkeepers.

■ **Love Street, September 17th, 1977. St Mirren v Rangers. A pulsating 3-3 draw, littered with fouls and controversy on the pitch, and crowd trouble off the pitch. Situations like this were almost impossible to police with supporters of both sides pressed against the segregation fence, hell-bent on causing trouble.**

346

■ Even with segregation, matches in the 1970s and '80s were often disrupted by fighting, pitch invasions and missile-throwing. It was dangerous and attendances fell. This is another photo of St Mirren v Rangers, September 17th, 1977.

■ **Celtic v Rangers, September 14th, 1974. Passions always run high at Old Firm games. Keeping the two factions apart was a major operation. There was a narrow passageway between The Jungle and the Dalriada Street end (traditionally the away end) of Celtic Park, but it was still a heavily policed area.**

■ In the past, segregation for Old Firm games was flexible. The games shown here weren't all-ticket, so police had to quickly adjust where supporters sat, and the position and width of the segregation divide, depending on how many supporters of each side showed up. The photo above is May 14th, 1983. The crowd was 40,500. Celtic had a chance of winning the league. They had to beat Rangers (which they did, 4-2) and hope Dundee would take a point at home to Dundee United (which they didn't). The Celtic support turned up in numbers and was given the Broomloan Road stand, some of the main stand and enclosure (a non-seated area at that

point) and a lower-tier section of the Govan stand. The photo on this page is the same year, but a new season – November 5th, 1983. A 2-1 win for Celtic. Managerless Rangers weren't having a vintage year but more of their support came out for this game. The crowd was 42,000. With fewer Celtic supporters in attendance the Govan Stand segregation divide has moved, is significantly wider, and is patrolled by more police. This would be unlikely to happen nowadays. Police and football authorities now insist upon ticketed games and wouldn't be willing to set a segregation divide then move it or alter the width of it several times.

■ Celtic 1, Rangers 2. August 23rd, 1980, in front of 58,000. It was rare for Celtic to move fans from The Jungle to create a wider segregation gap. But this game was different. It was closely monitored, and not just by football authorities. It was the first Celtic-Rangers meeting since the Cup Final riot three months earlier (See Violence chapter in Volume 3). There had been dark threats about government-imposed fines, closed-door games, and unspecified "even more swingeing sanctions", if a repeat of such disturbances was seen.

■ **Rangers 0, Celtic 0, on August 25th, 1984. This became the more usual set-up at Ibrox for an Old Firm encounter and it remained this way for years. Police keep a close eye on both sets of fans, who are confined to separate stands with adequate space between them.**

354

■ While the behaviour that led to a need for segregation was ridiculous, fervent and partisan support is a good thing – if controlled properly. Indeed it is what makes the atmosphere at big games "electric" (as match commentators love to say). The photo above shows tens of thousands of Celtic supporters at Ibrox on January 7th, 1978. Opposite: tens of thousands of Rangers supporters at Celtic Park, March 25th, 1978. The intensity of Old Firm encounters is famous throughout the football world. Or, at least, it used to be. Nowadays, for

League games, the clubs restrict fans of their rivals to small numbers. There is still loud support, of course, but without significant support for the other side it all flows one way. The clubs will say that with so many season books sold, there just isn't the room to accommodate thousands of visiting supporters because every season ticket holder must be guaranteed a seat for every game. And that's a fair argument. It is also true, however, that the spectacle of Old Firm encounters in years gone by was a very different thing.

■ Motherwell v Aberdeen, September 10th, 1983. The score in the game is hardly relevant to this photo, though it was 1-1 for anyone who is interested. The rise of "casuals" made the policing of segregation divides even more difficult. Young men not wearing club colours entered opposition areas to cause trouble. One is being arrested in this photo. There was always particular antipathy between Motherwell and Aberdeen casuals, both clubs had large groups. Hibs also had a particularly notorious gang throughout the 1980s.

■ Pittodrie, October 28th, 1972, Aberdeen v Celtic.

That's a knife speared into a 16-year-old girl's head.

The girl was, thankfully, allowed home from hospital that same evening after receiving treatment.

It takes an especially cowardly idiot to take a kitchen knife to a football match with the intention of throwing it.

This is why fans had to be kept far apart inside grounds. This is why football grounds had to change.

Thanks

THIS book has been the most enjoyable project I've worked on. I came to regard the many people who helped along the way as friends rather than colleagues.

There is nothing better, when doing what is supposed to be work, to find that you've just spent half an hour talking and reminiscing about fitba in the old days – and have forgotten what it was you were talking about in the first place. I am very grateful for the help, advice, expertise, and cups of tea.

The photos in this book are valuable artefacts of Scottish history. I am proud to bring them into the light. This is where I, and hundreds of thousands like me, grew up. We stood on those terraces, we watched our heroes, we enjoyed the experience with our friends and families around us. Going to the fitba in the old days was fantastic. I wish I'd appreciated it more at the time.

Since doing the first *Lifted Over The Turnstiles* book, I have been proud to get out around Scotland to speak to Football Memories groups. There is excellent work being done by an army of volunteers. When I show slides of old grounds and players, it quickly becomes apparent that I am not telling anyone anything – they are telling me! The greatest store of football knowledge that exists is held within the memories of the people who saw it happen. I am extremely grateful to have had some of that knowledge shared with me.

Heartfelt thanks for this, and various other reasons, are due to:

Craig Brown and Leanne Crichton for fantastic, insightful, generous forewords.

Leon Strachan (artist extraordinaire).

John Litster and Jock Gardiner (chief readers. Thanks for saving me embarrassment untold, guys).

Brian Wright (a fitba man of note).

Jim Kidd (almost solely responsible for the "Real Football" chapter).

Jim Burns and Norrie Rush (Hearts info, and lots more. I am truly in awe of their fitba knowledge).

James Coutts, Tony Fimister and Bill Gilby (Raith Rovers).

Bill Lilliman (English photos).

Mike Floate (of footballgroundsfrenzy).

Don Burnett (programmes expert).

Robert Dalzell (Airdrieonians).

David Walker (sports editor of The Sunday Post. Knows his fitba does David).

Joe Bloggs (Celtic Wikki. Good lad).

@StutheJag (Partick Thistle).

Seamus Ferry (Third Lanark).

Paddy Barclay (clever bloke, Paddy).

Tom Purdie (all-round Scottish football knowledge).

John Livingston (Kilmarnock).

The professors of the Old Scottish Football Pictures group on Facebook.

Michael White (Falkirk).

Robert Blackwood Strachan, 1926-2000 (Boghead).

Stuart Graham (Motherwell).

David Allan (Cowdenbeath).

Steve Gracie (Dundee United).

Martin Johnston

The Arab Archive.

Peter Hurn (of petespicturepalace)

Norrie Price (Dundee FC).

Doug Nicolson and Duncan McLean (speedway).

David Stuart (Scotland Epistles).

Kevin Robertson (Clyde).

Sue Shepherd (Pittodrie).

Paul Claydon (Groundstastic magazine).

Chris Gavin (Aberdeen).

Iain Harrison (Hibby).

Scott Husband.

George Ross.

Uli Hesse.

Douglas Tott.

Chris McNulty.

Ian Moffat.

Ian Stewart.

Alexander Hood.

George Yule.

Dennis McLeary (Berwick Rangers).

Colin Robertson.

Rob Casey.

Dave Piggot (for his knowledge of First Aid arrangements at football matches).

Kevin Robertson.

Alex Holmes.

David Mason.

Duncan Carmichael.

David Potter.

Iain McCartney.

Robert Weir.

The DCT archive is where all the gems are hidden. It is curated by a team of clever (and hard-working) people, led by David Powell, and comprising: Barry Sullivan, Gary Thomas, Irina Florian, Kirsty Smith, Katie Thompson, Melissa Lonie, and Mollie Horne.

Publishing a book is a lengthy process with input from many clever people who are very good at their jobs.

Craig Houston.

Gill Martin.

Sylwia Jackowska.

Jacqui Hunter.

Ryan Law.

Connor Vearnals.

Edward Wright.

Julie-Ann Marshall.

Chris Phin.

Nikki Fleming.

James Kirk.

Personal thanks to Carole, Rebecca and Lewis Finan. My family. Thanks for putting up with me and my ever-expanding collection of old football autobiographies.

Bill and Chris Nicoll.

David Patterson (Two Ts – got it right this time mate!)

Bob Seith (even though you don't like fitba!)

My oldest friend Frank Chalmers who went to so many games with me.

Brian Strachan, Doug Robertson, Dave Duncan and Richard Fenton, who shared football with me as a young daftie.

Fraser T. Ogilvie.

And lastly, my father, David Finan (1920-2012).

He first took me and my brothers to watch football all those years ago. He started my love affair with the beautiful game. I wish, beyond anything else on earth, that you were still here dad.

Other titles in the *Black & White Era* series

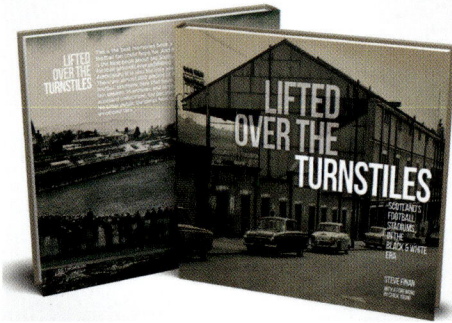

Lifted Over The Turnstiles Volume 1: Scottish Football Grounds in the Black & White Era

Rangers in the Black & White Era

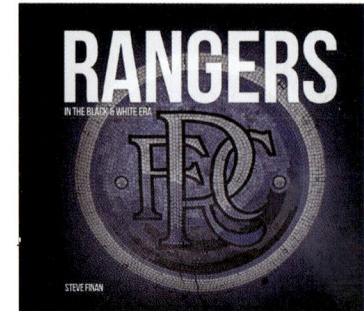

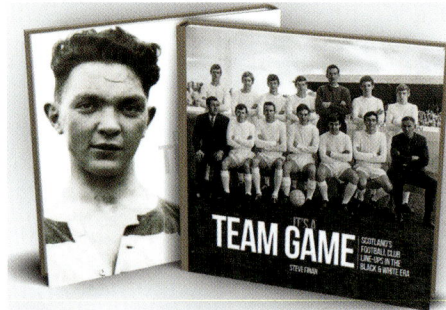

It's A Team Game: Scottish Football Club Line-Ups in the Black & White Era

Celtic in the Black & White Era

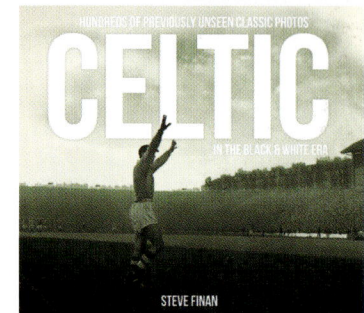

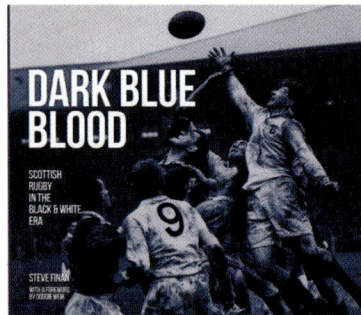

Dark Blue Blood: Scottish Rugby in the Black & White Era

Coming soon: **Scottish Golf in the Black & White Era**

Jim McLean: Dundee United Legend

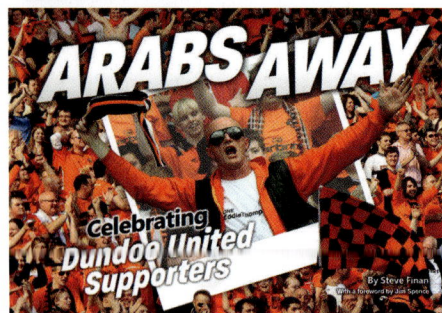

Arabs Away: Celebrating Dundee United Supporters

The Red Army: Celebrating Dons Supporters

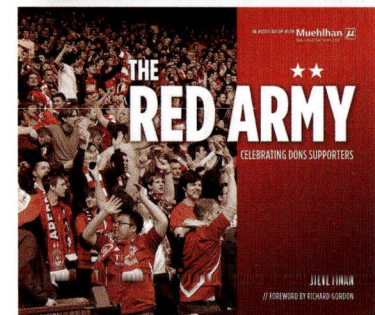

All titles available from dcthomsonshop.co.uk
Freephone 0800 904 7260